BECOMING A
PUBLISHED
Author

Agony and Ecstasy of Writing a Book

EVAN AND LOIS SWENSEN
and Many Fine Authors

ISBN 978-1-59433-340-8
eBook ISBN 978-1-59433-341-5

Manufactured in the United States of America.

Dedication

Dedicated to writers who have what it takes to become a published author. You have my greatest respect and admiration.

Contents

Introduction
Evan and Lois Swensen

More than three decades ago we wrote and published *Bringing Your Book to Market*, a small book describing how we create books and treat authors. We have not updated the book since. It has stood as the outline for our book publishing business. A few months ago we realized that we needed to remodel the book and bring it current with the times and include things like eBooks, which were not even invented when we first published *Bringing Your Book to Market*.

We determined that we'd include a few published authors' experiences to illustrate some of the publishing procedures employed to create a book and bring it to market. The more we talked with authors about what we wanted to do, the more we realized that *Bringing Your Book to Market* was pretty sterile, like most business plans. We also came to know that that's the way it should be, but there was a great need for a book with real experiences about becoming a published author. A book that would tell unpublished authors about the agony and ecstasy of writing a book.

We asked some of our author to write their story. The story they would like to have read prior to their journey to becoming a published author. Authoring and publishing a book is a daunting experience. Bringing, and keeping, a book before potential readers is a challenging and taxing undertaking. Almost everyone has dreamed about writing a book—but few there are that have what it takes to do it. Those who gave us their story had a vision of being a published author and had what it took to make it happen.

Becoming a Published Author: Agony and Ecstasy of Writing a Book contains the stories of real writers just like you. It's not the details. The details are written in *Bringing Your Book to Market. Becoming a Published Author* is the human side of publishing. It's the heart and the soul of authorship. It's the thrill of holding your newly published book and smelling the drying ink. It's the heart beating experience of seeing your book on a bookstore shelf. It's the dark day when you receive your manuscript back from the editor dripping in red ink. It's the agony of rewrites and rewrites; of book signings where no one shows up; of the morning you took all day to correct one sentence, only to take all afternoon changing it back to the way it was in the first place; of the Friday you gave up and declared yourself a writing failure. It's the ecstasy of the following Monday when you're energized with a breakthrough idea that propels you forward with vision and determination; of the fan mail from a perfect stranger telling you they read your book and loved it, and compared your writing to a famous author—past or present. Becoming a published author gives you celebrity status with both writers and readers; but, particularly among published authors who share your agony and ecstasy.

If you've written a book, if you're writing a book, or if you're thinking about writing a book, contact Publication Consultants. We invite you to become a published author with your own agony and ecstasy story.

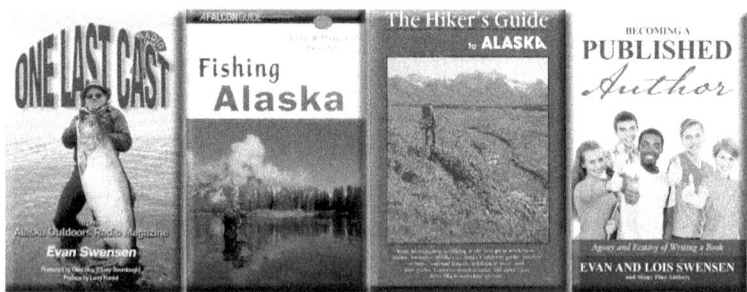

I Had Given Up Hope
Douglas Anderson

Publishing a book is easy. You make copious notes, collect all sorts of data, and finally sit down to write. The ideas pour forth faster than you can assign the words to paper, and soon you have your manuscript ready to submit to a publisher. You are convinced it's destined to become a bestseller. It's all so easy. Or is it?

In 1977 my company moved me from Montreal, Canada, to Alaska in support of the Trans Alaska Pipeline. For several years, I traversed the pipeline – in all seasons – from Prudhoe in the north to Valdez in the south and viewed lots of wild and spectacular country. I was certainly hooked on Alaska. Eventually I started flying, hiking, and gold prospecting with a very good friend. For a few memorable years we embarked on wilderness adventures that few ever have a chance to experience. Then, in 1985 my friend went to pursue a degree at the University of Hawaii and, shortly thereafter, my company relocated me to Atlanta, Georgia. Unfortunately, along with relocation, my adventurous lifestyle underwent a dramatic change for the worse and I was unsettled and none too happy at having been coerced to leave Alaska.

In my new position I traveled extensively and spent many hours on long flights and lonely nights in hotels, motels, or less desirable accommodations in unfamiliar places. To pass away the time and to alleviate my feelings of homesickness—and sometimes anger—I started to write about my Alaska adventures. Initially, I had no thoughts of writing a book. It was simply therapy and my way of reliving the experiences of flying, hiking in the wilderness, and the excitement of prospecting for that elusive gold. Sometimes I found myself laughing at a particular situation I was writing about – occasionally shedding a tear or two as well. Over a period of years I added more to the manuscript and it finally dawned on me that I had the makings of a pretty interesting book. I therefore set about word-processing my rough tome into a more logical form with chapters and headings.

I began to research ways to have my book published and very quickly realized it can be both complicated and expensive. Many publishing companies will not even consider looking at your manuscript simply because you are an unknown writer. I became disheartened and decided that my writing had served its purpose and it would go no further than my own bookshelf. The manuscript began to gather dust, though I picked it up occasionally and tinkered with it as a reminder of more exciting times.

Happily, in 1995—having spent ten years in Georgia—I found a way to return to Alaska. I felt I was returning home and also was happy to be back in support of the pipeline. Within a few months I became aware of Publication Consultants and was introduced to Evan Swensen. Evan appraised my manuscript and encouraged me to shake the dust off it once and for all. Maybe it could be turned into a real book if I could tidy it up just a little more. Of course, it was already organized and had been honed so many times I believed it was pretty near ready for the printing press.

My manuscript—word-processed to the best of my ability—was passed to the Publication Consultants editor then returned to me a couple of weeks later. I guess, up to that point, I thought I was a pretty fair writer. However, all of the cryptic red squiggles, dashes, punctuations, and deletions of superfluous words and even entire paragraphs, convinced me I had a long way to go. It's one thing for us aspiring authors to put ideas to paper but it takes a professional to turn that into something others can read and enjoy. Formatting deems there should be no long dragged-out sentences. There can only be so many lines to a page, so many pages in the book. All those *orphan* words sitting alone on the last line of a paragraph have to be eliminated and a chapter can't end with two lonely lines on an otherwise blank page. A writer's style may even be compared with Hemingway—though I never did like his style. And so it goes.

I worked on the suggested grammatical and punctuation changes and Publication Consultants worked out the final details. Within twelve weeks from signing an agreement, and Evan taking command, my book *Gold in Trib 1* was in many of the bookstores around Anchorage. I figured I had gone "national" when a friend found *Gold in Trib 1* on the shelf in the Walmart store in Plattsburg, New York and another friend took several to England and Scotland.

Evan was not satisfied. He soon pointed out that I had left myself wide open to writing a sequel to *Gold in Trib 1*. It took a little while to convince me but I eventually authored *Mystery in Trib 2* and Publication Consultants once again took it to press. It is said: "practice makes perfect." I think there was less editing necessary on this second book.

Publication Consultants arranged for occasional book signings and a group of authors would get together at some location. It was enjoyable, we encouraged each other, and had fun. It was certainly the best way to sell books.

With two books in print I thought I was finished with writing books. In 2001 my wife and I *retired* to Vancouver Island, British Columbia. Leaving Alaska again was a difficult decision but my consulting work was tapering off and I was working more at locations in the Lower 48 states. Undoubtedly Alaska was still in my bones. In 2009 I surprised Evan by writing a third book entitled *Lost in a Foreign Land* which picked up a link from the earlier books. Publication Consultants kindly took that to press as well.

One can take pride in being a "published author" no matter what the theme. We may never become rich – very few authors do – but there's much satisfaction in knowing that we achieved something that only a very small percentage of people manage to do and that our books will withstand the passage of time.

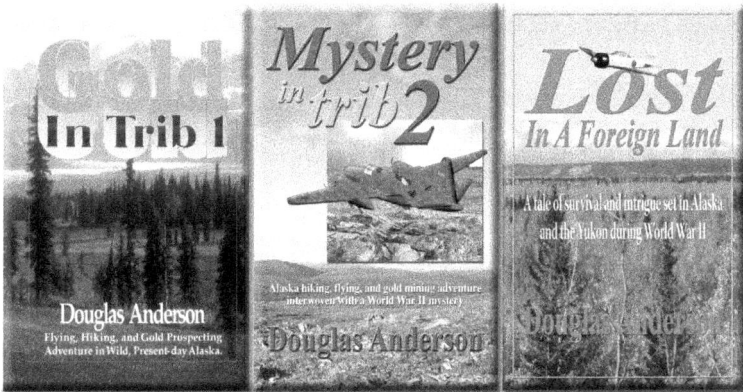

My Journey to Walter's Story
Barbara J Atwater

"So, what are you going to do with all this information you are gathering?" he asked me. I was speaking with a history professor from Oregon at a friend's party. My friend, Judy, knew of my interest in history and had introduced us. I was excitedly telling him how a genealogy project had gotten me so intrigued that I was spending a lot of time researching the history of the Pedro Bay area. I would find out something that would lead me on to another tidbit of history that was more exciting and intriguing than the one that lead me there. It was like a treasure hunt and I kept finding new clues to lead me on.

It was a good question. At the time, I hadn't considered what I was going to do with the information. I was just enjoying the searching. It was to be a few more years before I had the courage to actually think that maybe I had enough for a book. But how was I to do that? What would be the format?

It was around this time that I began to regularly visit Walter and Annie Johnson. They were full of the old lore of my home area. It really started when I asked Annie to help me with a cemetery project. I was trying to identify all those buried in the cemetery at Pedro Bay—graves were unmarked and many were difficult to locate. Annie and another elder, Mary Jensen, assisted me with this. We made a list of the people they knew were buried there. We came up with more people than there were identifiable graves. And, of course, I needed to know as much information about each person on the list as they were able to tell me—so many more leads and clues! As a result I found myself spending more time with Walter and Annie.

One day as I sat listening to Walter in his summer home in Pedro Bay, it dawned on me that maybe I could write this history through Walter. The more I listened to him, the more I realized what a truly unique life he had lived. He was the youngest of his family but was raised very much like an only child. His mother of Dena'ina/Russian descent only spoke the Dena'ina(language) in their home. She passed on to him much of the Dena'ina lore. Walter was a treasure house of the Dena'ina Indian culture and language of the area. He had a wonderful memory of so many characters that lived in the area. I did not say anything to him immediately. I needed to digest this idea myself first. Finally, one day I did speak to him of what I wanted to do. He looked at me and said I was too late. My heart sank. He told me about a book that Kari from the University of Alaska Fairbanks did with him. He showed me the book, *Sukdu Nel Nuhtghelnek I'll Tell You A Story* and I was amazed. It is a very good book. But it was very different from what I wanted to do. It is more of a scholarly work, focusing on the Dena'ina language. But Walter felt like there was no need for another book.

I recruited his daughter Ruthie to help me convince Walter that another book was possible. She had actually given me a lead in with the forward she wrote for *Sukdu Nel Nuhtghelnek I'll Tell You A Story*. "Another book in itself could be made from Dad's stories just about checking the trap line during the winters." Needless to say, we did convince him. He decided that perhaps there was more to tell.

So we started our journey in earnest! Walter lived in Homer and I lived in King Salmon. This meant a lot of travel. Every trip to Anchorage meant a side trip to Homer for my son, Ethan, and me where I recorded Walter's stories. Then I would transcribe the tapes. This went on for some years and finally I decided that I had enough and started to figure out how to put it together into a cohesive story.

Walter told me his stories as he remembered them not as they happened. I needed to organize the information, most of which I had to rewrite. It was very important to me to keep his voice, so I would write and then read it and listen to determine if I could hear him saying it in the way I had written it. After listening to him for so many years, plus listening to the tapes as I transcribed them, it was not too hard to do—to hear his voice in my head. So hopefully I have been successful in keeping his voice throughout this story.

Many more visits to Walter were required as I wrote his story, as additional questions were raised and needed clarification. Often he told me things in bits and pieces, as he remembered them and so it was like a puzzle. I needed to get everything and everyone connected in the right way.

It was here that I made another decision about this story. At first I had thought I would interview other family and friends to add to or flesh out Walter's Story. While working on the rewriting of his words I realized that this was indeed Walter's Story. To bring others in would, I felt, muddy the story. So what I did was include many endnotes that I hoped would help to further explain anything Walter either did not remember, or did not explain very well. In these endnotes I included some anecdotes from other people that I felt provided clarification on some of the characters and events. It was here, too, in the endnotes that I was able to include much of the research that I had been doing over the years.

I especially like the Distant Memories that precede each chapter of the book. These are all Walter's as told to him by his mother and other elders of the area. They are, I believe, an important part of the folklore of the Dena'ina people, the oral history of the area.

I am not a Dena'ina speaker and it was difficult at times to find an English word for a Dena'ina word that Walter used. In some cases, I thought it best to use the Dena'ina word but often could not determine what it was. Even with the use of Kari's fairly exhaustive Dena'ina language dictionary I was stumped. One such case was Walter's word for the invisible people. Because I couldn't find anything that seemed right I decided it best to use a blank for this word.

For the photos I owe my thanks to all those who were willing to share with me. It was hard to pick and choose which to use. Most, of course, are Walter's. I especially like Walter's sketches. The photos and Walter's illustrations definitely help to tell the story.

Because the people are so intricately connected in so many ways, I included several genealogies. It is my hope that some of the readers would be able to determine how they are connected to the area through these.

Yes, it has been quite a journey. There were many times that I would get bogged down and become discouraged. But, then someone would ask me how it was going. It would always seem to be just the impetus I needed to get back at it! So I am thankful to those who took the time and interest to inquire about my project—they don't realize how helpful that was!

I am so grateful to all those that helped me to believe that I could do this. One does not accomplish such an enormous task without a lot of help and encouragement. At a gathering some years ago, my brother looked directly at me and said, "Someone needs to write a history of this area." I thank, Norman, for the confidence he placed in me with those words, the confidence and vision to complete this project. I am grateful to the professor for asking me the question, to the friend who introduced me to him. I am especially grateful to my husband and son for their unwavering encouragement and support. Plus, it always seemed that just as I needed it, someone would appear to help me over a hurdle. So, yes, I am grateful for all the help along the way.

When I was finally ready for a publisher I went online and started searching. I compared services and prices. Those that were out of state were quite a bit cheaper but I really wanted someone close that I could deal with. Publication Consultations had many options so I went and talked with them in person. This was very helpful. Mr. Swensen showed me other books they had published and what some of the possibilities were. After this meeting I decided to go with them and have been thankful that I did. I have been quite pleased with their assistance through this process.

It was so exciting when the books arrived! My son was with me as we tore open a box to look at the finished product. It was a bit surreal, I must say. I immediately planned a Book Release Party at my house several weeks after the books arrived. It was a wonderful experience. Walter and his daughter and granddaughter were able to come. The event was celebratory and I truly appreciated each person that came, bought a book, and visited with me and with each other. Some even brought me flowers! One lady brought me a gift of fresh bread and homemade jam. I felt pretty special that day.

The reception of the book has been more than I could have anticipated. I found that I enjoy the marketing side of the book more than I thought I would, it is a totally new challenge. I am very much an introvert and so was dreading that part. Yet, I am finding I enjoy talking to people about the book. It is a whole new world for me, scary yet exciting.

It was a very long journey, and like most journeys had many hurdles along the way. But as I stated there were many along the way to help me keep going. I am very thankful and feel so blessed to have been able to complete my project—my journey to *Walter's Story*.

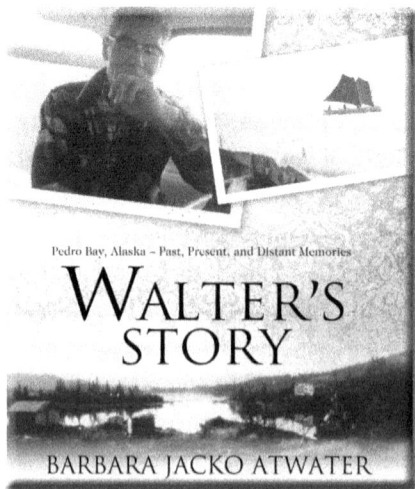

Returning, to Write My Novel
Jeff Babcock

What has been my experience on the road to becoming a published author? Not an easy question for me or, I assume, for any author to answer. The first step in my journey was to get my story down on paper, which surprisingly took me the better part of my adult life. My reluctance happened for a very good reason—something most young authors never realize until they have reached old age. In order to assimilate the truth behind many experiences, I believe it is necessary to view those experiences from the perspective of old age, unless of course you are born gifted. William Wordsworth captured this very human revelation in his poem *Ode on Intimations of Immortality from Recollections of Early Childhood* . . .

> We will grieve not, rather find
> Strength in what remains behind;
> In the primal sympathy
> Which having been must ever be;
> In the soothing thoughts that spring
> Out of human suffering;
> In the faith that looks through death,
> In years that bring the philosophic mind.

My understanding of what happened to me in the summer of 1967 was truly enhanced only after reflecting upon those *recollections* from my past through the eyes of an older and perhaps wiser version of myself.

Nevertheless, I first started writing about my adventure on Mount McKinley in the fall of 1967, about a month after I had returned to the east coast from what many have described as North American mountaineering's worst climbing disaster, a tragedy that took the lives of seven young men.

The Joseph Wilcox disaster was front-page news not only in Alaska and the Lower-48, but also in many newspapers around the world. I still have a collection of clippings stashed in a manila folder in one of my desk drawers.

When I got back to Connecticut in the fall of 1967, I received a phone call from the sports editor of the *New Haven Register*. He wanted to interview one of the survivors, who was also a member of the rescue team that found three frozen corpses up around the 19,000-foot level on the icy slopes of Denali.

Mount McKinley was renamed after our 25th President in 1878 by prospector William Dickey; the massive mountain with two distinct peaks was originally called *Denali* by the Dena'ina Athabascan people who inhabited the land surrounding the great mountain long before the encroachment of the civilized world. Denali means *The High One*. In 1967, fewer than two hundred people had ever been to the top of Mount McKinley. Our expedition was the 53rd attempt. As of today, more than 32,000 people have attempted to climb McKinley; a little more than half have reached the top.

Upon returning to my home in Connecticut after the tragedy, New England's autumn leaves were showing their full blaze of vibrant colors. By the time they had faded a month and a half later, I had returned to Nasson College in Springvale, Maine to start my sophomore year. The landscape had turned a barren gray by Thanksgiving holiday, yet I still remember my excitement when I discovered a complete set of slides from our Denali climb had arrived in the mail from my brother in Anchorage.

Before our first snowfall, the vivid memories of what I endured on Denali were once again alive in my mind. As a chilly afternoon wind scattered leaves across our backyard, I sat upstairs in my bedroom and carefully assembled each slide into one of the carousels from our family's Kodak slide projector. These tangible images triggered a myriad of reflections in my mind. Later that evening after dinner I began relating my adventure to my mother and my older brother Reggie as the larger images clicked across a barren wall in our living room. This was the first of hundreds of presentations I would make over the next several years. With each retelling, I found myself refining the details, which I felt would make my story more unique. What I had endured on the icy slopes of Denali was truly extraordinary and most people were virtually blown away as my story reached its climax. My adventure on Denali became a crowd pleaser, and I knew one day I would write a book about coming face to face with the Grim Reaper.

In the years that followed I attempted many times to pen the adventure of my life, but I was always disappointed with the end product. After college I became employed as a sophomore English teacher at Fitch Senior High School in Groton, Connecticut. A teacher down the hall offered to help me write my "novel." In fact, he wanted to pen the story himself, with the details provided by me. Frank Smith was already a published author, and writing an entire book seemed to me overwhelming and well beyond my level of skill as a writer. Yet, after a few months it soon became clear to me if anyone was going to write my tale of "Death on Denali," it would have to be me.

After a year of teaching on the east coast, a new development slowly began to creep into my life, almost as if I was starting my climb up Denali all over again. I felt as though something was missing—my life seemed pointless, as though I was just spinning my wheels, without any real sense of purpose. I was restless, unhappy, even disillusioned with the way things were going for me, so I decided to pack up my 1967 Pontiac station wagon with all my belongings and say goodbye to my home in Connecticut. Like Percival searching for the Holy Grail, I began my second great quest traveling alone across the states and up into the Canada; finally I forged my way up the Alcan Highway all the way to Anchorage. Clearly my adventure on the Last Frontier four years earlier was beckoning me to return to the place where my sense of manhood had been tested and the so-called bridge between adolescence and adulthood had been successfully crossed, or at least so I thought.

The years passed quickly—after a variety of jobs, new friends and relationships, and the furthering of my education—I became a special-education elementary school teacher. Along the way I had honed my skills as a mountaineer and had become an assistant outdoor education instructor in Anchorage Community College's mountaineering program.

Admittedly a late bloomer, I eventually fell in love and within a few years I was married and a father of two children. Then around year seven, the terrible reality of divorce came into my experience—a story not unique to me, and perhaps similar to many. Yet, in spite of this great sadness, my desire to write slowly began to emerge from the recesses of my mind.

As it turned out my divorce proved to be one of those mixed blessings that open the door to a whole new dimension. While my children lived with their mother during the school year, I discovered time to reflect upon the past several years of my life. What had happened to me? Why was my world falling apart just when I thought everything was going my way?

The proverbial self-help therapies of the '70s and '80s became my lifeline. And yes, I tried everything from psychotherapy and working with a Jungian analyst to many of the other "new age" approaches, which promised to help me *help myself*—an Elizabeth Kubler-Ross externalization workshop, weekly meetings of the Adult Child of an Alcoholic (ACOA) group, M. Scott Peck and his *Road Less Traveled* book series, which culminated in my attendance at one of his *Community Building workshops*, Leonard Orr's and Sondra Ray's "rebirthing-breathwork" techniques aimed at helping me to experience and heal suppressed emotions from my birth, and finally the eastern practice of daily meditation.

Yes, I had suppressed many negative emotions and experiences from my childhood. Yet rather than maintain a practice of *denial*, which most of my family adhered to, I decided to release a few of the skeletons from our family's closet.

So my climb up Mount McKinley in 1967 became a bit more than your average "Me-and-Joe climbed a mountain" story. *Should I Not Return* was quickly turning into my autobiography and into the story of two brothers who believed they had escaped to Alaska and left behind the shadows from their past.

In fact, my book is a testament to anyone who has ever dabbled in "life-threatening" activities like mountain climbing—trying to escape those repressed feelings from childhood. Such addictive behaviors akin to drug, alcohol, or substance abuse certainly fall into the same category.

Disorders which are sexual in nature, or those triggered by obsessive-compulsive (OCS) impulses in the brain, can also be viewed in the same light. These *acting-out* behaviors may offer a euphoric sense of pleasure or a feeling of escape from painful associations in the past, yet any psychiatrist will tell you such addictions do nothing to heal the origin of those festering wounds. In the Arthurian myth, these real-life repressions of human angst are commonly referred to as the "Fisher King wound."

As I began to comprehend and dig into some of these roots from my past, I found myself wanting to somehow put these thoughts into my novel. And my recollection of coming face to face with death on Denali seemed not only a good place to start, it also seemed the most logical. What better place to shed some light on my past than to visit the icy, storm-blasted upper slopes of "The High One," once again. In my mind it felt like I was coming to terms with God Almighty or Satan himself.

So I again began writing. Over the course of the next several years, I penned three different screenplay versions of the story—*Archdeacon's Tower*, was followed by *Divine Fate*, which was then updated into a version I called *Nature's Edge*. Then, for a full year I tried to garner the interest of an agent or manager in Los Angeles, to get my screenplay made into a blockbuster film.

Then, one snowy night I became trapped in the coastal town of Whittier, Alaska. For several days I had been bartering back and forth over the Internet with a Mr. Michael Cushman of *Creative Entertainment Group* in Los Angeles. I awoke the following morning in my room at the Anchor Inn and discovered Mike was willing to take me on as a client! In his brief return email message, he complimented me on my newly revised synopsis, the "pitch" to my screenplay *Archdeacon's Tower* and he wrote: "Send me the spec, Jeff. What you have written is far superior to the other pitches you've sent. Let's see if we can get you a producer."

Four years went by in a flash with the expected nibbles and bites from various sharks and tadpoles swimming around the LA oceans, yet nothing ever panned out. In the meantime, I was given the name of a book publisher who was based in Anchorage by the name of Evan Swensen. Evan too was intrigued by my story, but he did not work with screenplays, so he encouraged me to transfer the story into a novelized format.

By now, I was approaching retirement from teaching in Alaska, and my wife and I decided to move to Green Valley, Arizona in 2007 to be near her then 92-year-old father in his later years. Although we have resided in Green Valley for nearly five years, I still managed to make at least one trip back to Alaska each year. The most recent journey this past summer was a joy, since it involved book signings and the promotion of my newly published novel, entitled *Should I Not Return*.

As to be expected, many developments have occurred in our lives during this time—my own health issues came into play, which involved surgery, then came the deaths of friends and relatives, the birth of our first grandchild, and of course the financial ups and downs, which coincided with the downfall of our economy. Throughout our time in Arizona, I wrote the novelized version of my story.

Several months were devoted to rewrites and revisions, during a recovery period from three separate cardiac incidents, and also from a full knee replacement surgery. Evan has been exceedingly helpful with the laborious process of getting my book published.

Yet, after my book was released to the public in April of 2012, I discovered one final step, which is perhaps the hardest part of an author's journey. Yes, bringing a book into the tangible reality is a difficult and time-consuming struggle, as this brief chapter about my experience certainly implies. Yet, the real struggle, namely *the promotion of an author's book*, is perhaps even more challenging. I established my own book's website address, which can be found at *www.shouldinotreturn.com*. With Evan's help we sent out galley copies to prospective reviewers who wrote glowing remarks about my book. I have a You-tube video posted on the Internet: *www.youtube.com/watch?v=h71WVl-wo3U*. In a similar vein, I visited hundreds of other sites, which offer ways to promote an author's work. Some of the advice was very helpful, and some not.

Publication Consultants too is doing their best to help authors with this crucial step in the book-publishing game by initiating an author's group on Google's website, in order to help his established authors communicate with each other and share their own experiences and ideas. They are also providing authors with opportunities to hear from professionals in the business who are willing to offer their advice via a webinar author's site sponsored by Publication Consultants.

In conclusion, a novel takes years of effort to complete 70,000 to

140,000 words. If you do decide to invest the necessary time into writing a novel, you will discover the long time it takes will be one of the greatest challenges you will ever face. One adage I've run across claims that out of every hundred people who start a novel, only three finish.

If your goal is to see if you can write that book you've been dreaming about, then by all means, give it a try. You won't know how you feel until after you begin to discover the joy of writing. Take it from me, it is not only therapeutic, it may turn into one of the best ways you will ever spend your time. As I have stated at the onset of this chapter, *Should I Not Return* took me the better part of my adult life to finish. Without a doubt I am very grateful I decided "to return" to the roots of my beginning. Completing my novel has been one of the most gratifying experiences of my life. Just remember, if you are interested in having people buy your book (other than just your friends or relatives), you will be facing another of the greatest challenges of your life—the fine art of promoting your book to the general public.

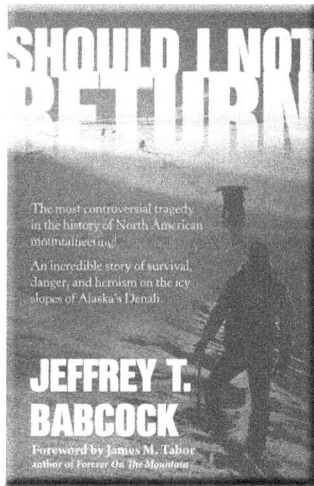

What's Next!
Jan Boylan

I had never even thought seriously about publishing a book, unless it was a children's book, and then it would need to be illustrated, and I wasn't a good enough artist. I wasn't a good enough writer either, and had no idea where to start.

Fast-forward to 2003. I was on the board of directors for the Senior Center, and chairman of the fund-raising committee. We needed a project to make money for the Center. I thought, gee, we have this huge number of senior citizens and many of them went through the 1964 earthquake in Anchorage. Maybe they would like to share their stories. If we copied them and put them together with a comb binder we might even be able to sell them at the Center for $10 each. The authors would at least buy one and that would pay for the paper, ink, and so forth, and maybe a little extra.

I put out a flyer at the Senior Center and asked for stories. They started coming in fast and furiously. I also got a call from Dolores Roguszka. I had no idea who she was, but when she offered to help I jumped at the opportunity to have some assistance. "Of course I would love the help!"

Then I went to talk to her and found her to be very intelligent, and she was also an author. She had written a book on photography 30 years before, but hey. She knew more than I did. She would edit the stories. Super!

So I gathered the stories, typed them up from bits of paper or from taped stories and interviews. Some came by email, and that made my job easier. We kept the email communications red-hot. I sent stories to Dolores for her final touches and editing. She also collected stories from her friends, many of whom were old-time Alaskans. Unfortunately, we couldn't use most of the stories verbatim because there was so much repetition—how many times could someone read about a kitchen floor covered with broken dishes, catsup, mustard, and honey—but Dolores knew how to cut and paste, and she worked very hard. Fortunately Jean Paal contacted Dolores and helped her with the editing, which gave her a much needed respite.

When we thought we had enough stories we talked about a name for the book, and how to organize the stories, what to use for the cover, and so on. Dolores definitely took the lead, as she was smarter about it than I was. Although we agreed before a topic was put to rest, so I did get in my two cents.

Before Dolores retired she had been a photographer, and had taken lots of pictures of the earthquake aftermath, so we decided to include many of her pictures interspersed throughout the book, and she had the lead story, which she had written right after the quake.

Stories typed and edited, pictures selected, title decided upon. Dolores wouldn't let me get away with the comb-binding idea. She said we needed a "real" book. Now we needed a publisher.

We went to the phone book and found some listings, took our papers and headed for the offices. The first publisher we went to wanted to know what we wanted. Since we really had no idea even what he meant, that wasn't very helpful. He showed us several books he had published, but that still didn't tell us anything we really needed to know. We were a little discouraged, and I talked to Elizabeth Tower, who I knew had published several Alaska history books. She suggested we talk to Publication Consultants.

What a difference! He told us what we did and what we didn't need to do, and we knew we had found what we were looking for. He helped us with decisions and guided us in the right direction. We received the first printing on Thanksgiving of 2004. They sold so fast we felt we needed to order a second printing right away. We doubled our order, but by March 2005 we still needed to send for a third printing, having sold the first two. We are now in our sixth printing, and couldn't be happier with his direction, and with the results of our efforts.

AND . . . the Senior Center has had money to pay many bills, and the money is still coming in, although not as quickly. It was a great project, and one I repeated on a different topic a few years later. All royalties from both books, *The Day Trees Bent to the Ground,* and *In the Light of the Night and the Dark of the Day* continue to benefit the Anchorage Senior Center.

I also published a pamphlet on bridge about the ABCs of bidding, entitled, *Bridge Bidding Made Easy.* It is a great aid in learning the bidding process.

Haven't decided what to do next. Maybe I'll write that children's book.

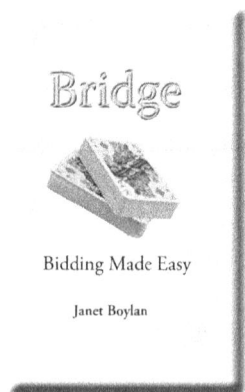

Stories from the '64 Alaska Earthquake

THE DAY TREES BENT TO THE GROUND

Compiled by Janet Boylan
Edited by Dolores Roguszka
Photographs by Dolores Roguszka

In the Light of the Night and the Dark of the Day

Tales of Alaskans at Work and Play

COMPILED BY JANET BOYLAN
EDITED BY JEAN PAAL
ILLUSTRATED BY ROBERT GILMORE
FOREWORD BY GEORGE SULLIVAN

Bridge

Bidding Made Easy

Janet Boylan

Getting in Harness
Pat Chargot

I worked as a journalist for almost three decades before writing a book— my first—for Publication Consultants. What took me so long? My nine-to-five job, of course. It's hard to find the time, let alone the creative stamina necessary to embark on a project as complex as a chapter book when you're reporting and writing news stories five days a week.

Unlike most of my colleagues at the *Detroit Free Press,* I was self-taught. I earned my spurs the hard way, in a climb that started at the very bottom of the ladder, as a secretary/receptionist in the paper's Features Department. In college, I had majored in English, and had stumbled into the news business by pure accident a month after I graduated. I like to say that I didn't choose journalism—it chose me. I was utterly unfamiliar with the profession, so I had to start small.

Did I say I started small? My first assignment was to compile the paper's weekly entertainment calendar—a list of hundreds of events with their corresponding dates, times, and admission prices—and I quickly learned the importance of fact checking. It was Journalism 101, to be sure, but it was new to me and I considered it a challenge.

Soon, I was writing one- and two-paragraph items for *Detroit,* the paper's glossy Sunday magazine. I cut my teeth at the magazine, graduating incrementally to longer and longer and more and more complex pieces, all the while struggling to write well with as much grace and proficiency as my more experienced colleagues. I struggled mightily, sweating blood over every story, searching for the right "lead" or first several paragraphs, paging through the thesaurus for snappy verbs, grasping for transitions until through dumb luck or sheer doggedness I would finally hit on *le mot juste*. Writing was hell, but it was so satisfying to finish a story, knowing that I had given shape to my thoughts to the best of my ability. I persevered and, lo and behold, over time—a very long time—I became a solid and versatile writer. And I had an idea for a chapter book (a book for young readers).

The idea germinated in 1999 on a trip to Alaska—my first—to cover the start of the Iditarod Trail Sled Dog Race for *Yak's Corner*, the paper's weekly news magazine for kids. Five years earlier, after 23 years of reporting and writing for virtually every department at the newspaper, I had shifted gears to become the *Yak's* lead writer, confounding my colleagues. I decided to write for kids in elementary school—50,000 of them in Detroit Public Schools alone—many lacking quality reading materials at home. It was an intuitive leap that turned out to be the right one for me, and I have never looked back.

Would I have written a book had I not made that leap? I have no idea, but writing for *Yak's Corner* definitely helped me to find my "voice" and unleashed my creativity with the intensity of a tropical storm in a rain forest. I reached into the rich well of my childhood and even into my emotional and spiritual lives and found freedom and authenticity. I reached deep in Alaska, where I stopped in at Iditarod headquarters in Wasilla and first heard about the dog who—I'm aware that I'm anthropomorphizing by using "who" instead of "that"—would become the subject of my book.

Balto was the lead sled dog on the final leg of a 1925 life-saving relay to carry serum from Fairbanks to Nome to save the town's children from diphtheria. The serum run is regarded as "the first Iditarod" and made the dog an overnight sensation—a BONEa fide international celebrity. After his death, Balto's body had been stuffed and mounted. But where was Balto's mount now? Not at Iditarod headquarters, where the mount of Togo, another famous Alaska sled dog, resided in a glass case. I asked about that and, upon learning that Balto's mount was in Cleveland, I decided to write a *Yak* story about Balto when I got home. The staff member who divulged this great secret had no idea how the mount had ended up in Cleveland. I would find out. Curiosity is a major ingredient of nonfiction writing—perhaps the most important ingredient.

Back in Detroit, I called the Cleveland Museum of Natural History and talked to Steve Misencik, an exhibits designer and fount of Balto esoterica. The museum displayed the mount every winter, around the time of the Iditarod. Thanks to Steve, the display had grown every year to include more and more information and artifacts. Steve's enthusiasm ignited mine and I ended up writing not one, but two stories about Balto. Yet, after they were published, I couldn't let the dog go—which isn't at all like me. Normally, when I finish writing a story, I move on to something else that strikes my fancy. But now, my interest was piqued: I daydreamed about visiting the museum's Balto archives to learn more. A few months later, at my own expense, I did, in hopes that I would find enough new and fascinating material for a book.

Steve recommended a wonderful B&B near the museum, where I ensconced myself for three days. We had a meal together and got to know each other, and I immersed myself in countless old newspaper articles and other documents about Balto and his peripatetic life in both Alaska and the Lower 48. I also visited *The (Cleveland) Plain Dealer*, which permitted me to dig through its numerous clippings about Balto. Best of all, Steve agreed to show me the mount, which was in storage at the time. The museum had taken good care of it and it was in excellent shape— and gorgeous! Balto's once black fur had turned the color of mahogany, but it was still thick and glossy. The stuffed dog had poise and presence, exuding something of the old Balto magic, of his charisma and spirit. I was smitten and knew absolutely that I would write a book.

I realized I would need to do more research and I reveled in it, working at night and on weekends for several months before I was ready to write. I treated the book like an investigative project, searching high and low for snippets of new information. The University of Michigan library borrowed rare books for me from libraries in other states (including Alaska and Massachusetts) about the serum run; Siberian huskies; Leonhard Seppala, a musher famous in Alaska's history and Balto's owner; Togo, Seppala's favorite dog, who was injured in the serum run; Roald Amundsen, the famous polar explorer, who knew Seppala and brought Balto's vaudeville tour across the Lower 48 to a screeching halt; Sol Lesser, the Hollywood producer who leased the dogs and made a reenactment film of the serum run; and several other major and minor figures in Balto's story. I even located Lesser's son, Bud, in California, who, in his eighties, recalled the dogs visiting his elementary school and "feeling like a hero" because they belonged to his father.

The more I learned, the more ambitious the project became. I was no longer satisfied to focus solely on Balto; I wanted to place the hero dog within the context of his times, recreating the feel of the many U.S. cities he visited, including a burgeoning Los Angeles and Hollywood, and a New York City teeming with immigrants. It was the wild, jazzy, fun-filled Roaring Twenties. Flappers in short skirts were kicking their legs and twirling the long strands of pearls they wore around their necks. The economy was booming—lots of people were making money and spending it on having fun. I wanted kids to learn about all that and one of my favorite periods in American history. I reported Balto's story into the ground, accumulating a mountain of compelling information, much of it unknown to most Americans, about one of the world's most famous dogs.

I was finally ready to write. I wrote all day Saturdays and Sundays, completing chapter after chapter until I crossed the finish line in a burst of exhaustion and elation, as if I had completed a marathon. In a way, I had. I was proud of my accomplishment, but I dreaded the even harder, perhaps impossible, job of finding a publisher. I sent the book to 10 New York publishers, thinking that because I wrote for one of the country's largest newspapers and by this time had an impressive resume, someone would snap it up. After all, I was a published professional writer, not a beginner.

I was wrong. What I really needed, I was told, was an agent—but, as it turned out, agents were even harder to find than publishers. Most agents didn't even respond to my submissions. I ended up with a pile of rejection letters from publishers—several of them complimentary, but no one was "interested at this time."

Then I had an idea: Why not create a Web site and post the book online? I was satisfied with the salary I made at the paper and didn't really need additional money. I simply wanted my book to be read by kids— hundreds of them, thousands of them. Hundreds of thousands had read my *Yak* stories; I wanted hundreds of thousands to read *The Adventures of Balto: The Untold Story of Alaska's Famous Iditarod Sled Dog*.

So I hired a local Web designer, who created a charming and kid-friendly online home for the book. I commissioned an artist friend to paint a portrait of Balto, using several historic photos as references; we put the portrait on the book's cover. I even had Balto postcards made up and mailed them to friends, announcing the site's launch. The project was pure fun; still, I longed to find a "real" publisher. Finally, I did— Publication Consultants—and it was a perfect fit.

I had seen one of their books in Anchorage, eventually thought to call, and found myself chatting with Evan, who, of course, knew all about Balto and was familiar with the legendary serum run. Publication Consultants specialized in books about Alaska, and soon asked to publish my book. How simple! I wish I had thought of it earlier, but then I wouldn't have launched my own Web site, which had been another brand-new experience.

Evan and Lois did a lovely job of turning my digital book into paper. They used the same cover, and also were able to include six historic photos, which really helped to bring Balto to life. I was thrilled to receive that first box of books; I buy replacement boxes regularly so that I always have copies on hand to give to new friends and acquaintances, especially kids and teachers. To me, being able to do that means a lot, though if lightning did strike someday and the book ended up on a best-seller list, I sure wouldn't mind.

I am now officially retired, but still work for the paper part-time as a freelancer (on contract and still as the *Yak's* lead writer). I hope eventually to write another book and, thanks to my first publishing experience, have the confidence to jump right in, plug away, and complete it once I know in my heart that I have found the right subject. I like to try fiction. It might be something for kids, but it will probably be a book for adults. That's the English major in me speaking; at the moment, my journalist self is quite content to yak weekly during the school year at www.yakscorner.com and write occasional pieces for www.readthespirit.com, an interfaith religion and spirituality site.

I learned so much by writing that first book. For me, it embodied the maxim from the *Tao Te Ching:* "A journey of 1,000 miles begins with a single step." I took a first step toward a book—drove to Cleveland to do research on Balto—and then a second, and a third . . . and hundreds of small steps and reached my goal. I see now that writing a book with an introduction, 23 chapters, and an epilogue isn't a lot different from writing 23 stories on the same subject—and I had had a lot of practice doing that, having produced numerous 24-page special projects for the *Yak* on presidential elections, foreign countries and more.

I think of my time spent writing *Balto* as a kind of Zen experience. I tried to stay in the moment—focus on the chapter I was working on and not worry about those that lay ahead. I dug deep in deciding how to start the story, and trusted my gut and intuition, as I do in writing for the newspaper. I did not write countless drafts. I wrote one, exactly as if I were writing for the paper, where deadlines make second and third drafts impossible. Instead, I worked on each chapter until I had it right, polishing sentences, deleting phrases and inserting better ones; rewriting sections that felt flat until they sang to me. At night, I'd read aloud to my husband what I had written that day, so I could hear how the sentences sounded.

Perhaps I should have been a sculptor or a musician. I love tinkering with and reworking what I have written, leaving each chapter I've honed to the best of my ability and moving on to the next one. No second drafts for me.

There were magic moments here and there, times when a word or a phrase or a transition would jump onto my computer screen so unexpectedly that I felt as if Balto himself were helping me tell his story, like some canine angel with wings! I should stop here before I write something truly silly, but I came to love that dog and his story, the conclusion of which brought tears to my eyes when I wrote it. That book is my little valentine to the universe, with a message for everyone—a message that I hope inspires readers of all ages.

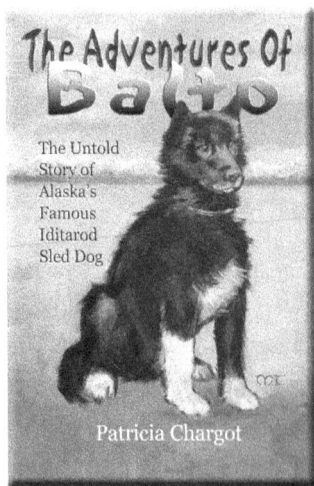

The Adventures Of Balto
The Untold Story of Alaska's Famous Iditarod Sled Dog
Patricia Chargot

Creating One Good Story at a Time
Halene Petersen Dahlstrom

Christmas Connections came into being during a time of tremendous family difficulties, deteriorating health, and the first Christmas after the sudden death of my oldest brother, Berdell. Though he had many struggles in his own life, he had always been a balm to my sagging spirits, and an enthusiastic supporter of my writing projects. Reminiscing about holidays past, especially those of my childhood, I remembered that when I was ten years old, I had lost a specially purchased Christmas gift—a package of hankies. I began to wonder what had happened to them, who had found them, if they had been used as a gift, or for personal need. From that thought Christmas Connections began to develop. It seemed as if I was watching a movie and writing down the scenes as I saw them. But it was by no means a fast-moving project.

Thankfully we were able to get a computer a year later, which made all the difference to the completion of Christmas Connections. Often when I was unable to sleep, I could focus on the story, what my characters were feeling, saying, etc., and put in a small-town, 1960s America setting, much like the one I grew up in.

The first time I thought it was finished, a few friends read it and liked it enough to encourage me. I sent it to a supposedly reputable editing service and shortly after they received my manuscript and requested a large sum of money, they went out of business. Luckily, I was able to stop payment on the check. This happened another time, and I grew to distrust writing-linked professionals, and to doubt my story's future.

About the third year, I started to revise the story. Another small book called, The Christmas Box by Richard Paul Evans was having success at that time, so I was encouraged to try again. When I felt my story was completed at this stage, a couple of family members read it and helped with editing. I sent it to three publishers and was of course—rejected.

More than a year later I decided to try again. Two new characters came into being, and the heavenly-connection tying the book together was formed. It didn't change the original story, just added another dimension. Then just as I was ready to do the last edit and spell check, my Word Perfect file melted down! It happened just as I was saving changes to disc, so my good disc copy was corrupted too. All I had left of the story was a copy without any of the last three month's revisions. Of course I felt sorry for myself, and began to listen to others who said, perhaps it was God's way of saying, "It's not your turn." Or, "It's not your time." I put the book away for two years. Then we moved to Alaska.

I can't remember why I decided to try again. Maybe I was prompted by the success of others, or, getting a boot from the other side. This time I began each writing opportunity with prayer, knowing that I would stand a better chance of succeeding with God in my corner. I tried to find moments to write that were the least contentious in my home, and played inspirational music softly in the background.

Did it work 100 percent? No. Did it create instantaneous harmony within my family? No. But it certainly helped! It also got me back on track whenever I walked away in frustration. During one of those times, I began praying to know if I was supposed to continue. I wondered if I was being selfish or if the timing still wasn't right.

A couple of days later, I went to a special church gathering at the temple. I went with the writing question in mind, but only secondarily. Mostly my focus was on the meeting. Then an interesting thing happened. Instead of lingering afterward to visit with other church members, as I usually would have done, I felt like I should leave. I rationalized … there is nothing pending at home, no one in dire need, why shouldn't I stay and enjoy visiting? The more I questioned this feeling, the stronger it got—leave! I did, but not with any great haste. I stepped outside, again questioning why I had felt prompted to leave. No answer came.

A woman was parked in front of the building, waiting for her husband. I noticed an old bumper sticker from my hometown, Riverton, Utah, and began to talk to her. It turned out that she had lived in Riverton but had left more than 40 years ago. I told her that I was new to Alaska and began asking her for suggestions on how to cook salmon. She was clearly a vast reservoir of knowledge. At this point, I decided that God must have wanted me to meet this lady so I would quit wasting fish, and I asked if I could call her.

She said yes and gave me her card. I read it and gasped—she and her husband own a publishing company in Alaska.

There was my answer ... go forth, it is time. I worked on my manuscript for another two months, and then just as I was ready to submit it ... the entire computer melted down, and not even the computer experts could put that dumpty back together again.

This time I had a back-up copy and after the UPS man delivered our new computer, I started the final edit. Or so I thought. Through the publisher I was introduced to a real live editor, Marthy Johnson. She is the Hope Diamond in world of cut-glass editors that I had previously worked with, and a great teacher. My story lost hundreds of words on the Marthy Johnson editing diet. But Christmas Connections is better for it.

So, it all ends happily ever after? Not quite yet. I have learned that there is more to writing and publishing than I ever imagined, and feel like I have just stepped off the merry-go-round and bought a ticket for the roller coaster. So hang on . . .

I received a lot of help at different stages and freely acknowledge this with tremendous gratitude. What I hope now is that people who read my book will want to read the next book in the series.

But most importantly, I hope that as you read Christmas Connections you will gain a renewed sense that our earthly experience is not a random happenstance or a cruel joke, but rather a planned, blessed event with eternal consequences that connects us in this world and beyond ...

The afterward above can be found on page 126 of Christmas Connections—miracles one good deed at a time. It recounts that after years of working on the story, juggling marriage, motherhood, moves, and maladies, it was finally published due to divine intervention and the timely meeting of Margaret Swensen, of Publications Consultants. Her encouragement finally got me on track to publication and the first edition of Christmas Connections came out in August of 2000. A month later, Margaret found out she had cancer.

Margaret Swensen was one of the loving examples I used to develop the character of Enid Watterson in this book. It's part of my tribute to her. What a valiant effort she made to stay on earth with her family and friends! But Heaven had other plans. Margaret died on February 6, 2002. At her funeral, I remarked to a friend, "Margaret Swensen opened the door for me with my writing." As soon as I said it, I felt wrapped in a warm glow and in my mind heard her voice say, "Yes, I opened the door for you—now don't you shut it!"

Writing is a challenge, a blessing, and a trial in my life. I continue to create my version of living and loving for my own amusement, and hopefully yours. I'm doing the best that I can to keep that door open. I heard you, Margaret—and thanks again!

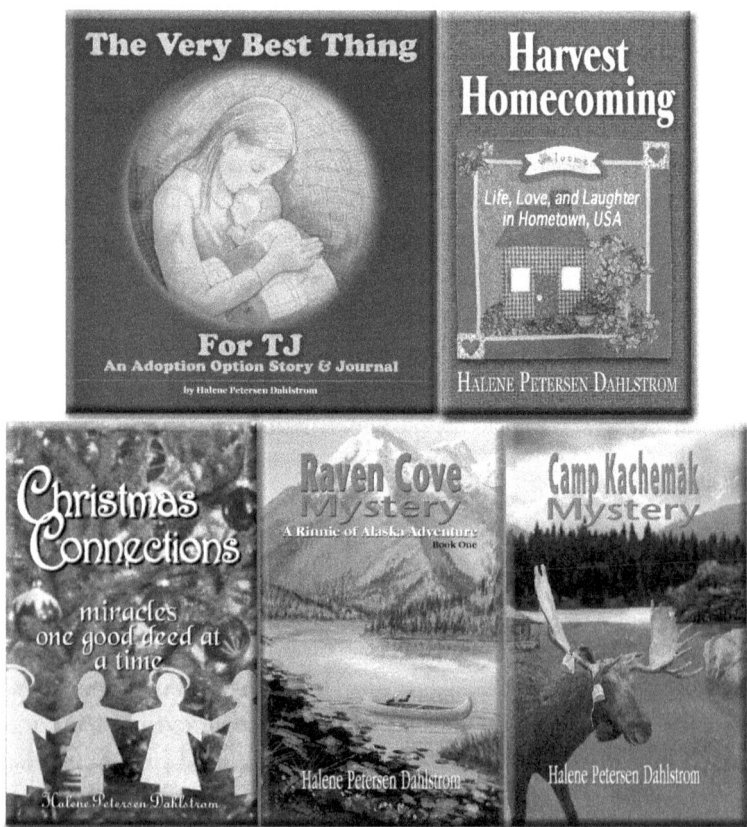

How Turtle in a Racehorse World Began
Kati Dahlstrom

One day I was upset about my life and my mom told me to start writing a book. I had wanted to start writing one anyway because I felt that it was not just my life and disabilities that needed to be addressed, but that others out there with disabilities felt the same way I do. It soon became a mission of mine. I had a lot to say, so I figured that I would just pour out my heart, even if afterward I wondered why I had written it in the first place.

The venting process started in 2004, and took more than four months to complete. Then the real work began! The venting had to be sorted, sentence by sentence, topic by topic, and chapter by chapter, in order to figure out what was worth keeping. My mom helped me with that. We had to decide what the gems were, and what was just gravel. From time to time I got confused thinking that the gravel were the gems that needed to be kept. Mom used plenty of humor and patience to help me see the difference.

Thank heavens for computers with the Cut and Paste feature! I learned more and more about myself, what was a real concern, and what was a temporary upset. I can honestly say that I see things a lot more positively now. I loved writing my book, and feeling like I might make a difference in the lives of other people. The only thing I didn't like was the fact that it took so blasted long in between the writing, the organizational process, the editing, and the publishing—more than four years! Now I understand all too well the frustrations other authors feel.

The first part of this book is about my life, frustrations, and feelings. The second part contains some of my favorite writing projects from over the years. I definitely plan to continue with my writing because once I start a project, there are so there are so many ideas going through my head that I can't wait to share.

I dedicated my book like this: To God, for giving me the inspiration; To my mom, for helping me with the editing, which took a great amount of patience and time; To my dad, for his dedication to his work, and support during the long haul; To Jeff, Colter, Janean, Jennalee, Danny, Weston, and Savanna, for giving me encouragement to carry on; To my extended family and friends who helped me with this project; To my teachers, my heroes, and all who have never given up on me; To the many doctors and other health professionals who have helped me throughout my life; And to my dogs, Libby and Shadow, for their constant love and companionship until the very end of their lives.

A special thanks goes out to Special Olympics and the ACE program for helping me realize my true potential and that I really do have a future if I am willing to work for it.

Writing this book has been an absolute joy for me, but it took lots of soul searching and perseverance. It has taught me a lot. I hope those of you who read it will feel the same way.

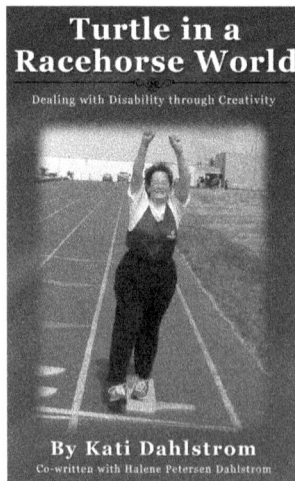

Turtle in a Racehorse World

Dealing with Disability through Creativity

By Kati Dahlstrom

Co-written with Halene Petersen Dahlstrom

Retired to Write
Carl Douglass

I spent ten years in research to produce my first book, *Last Phoenix*, and was altogether convinced that it was the new Great American Novel. However, literary agents, some 150 of them, were less sanguine about the book. More accurately, they were not interested in my query letter. Two read the book. One found it interesting, but not to her taste, and the other said it needed more work to make it professional. End of story.

I went hunting to Alaska, and as usual took my manuscript with me to tweak it. I met my nephew after the hunt and learned that he was the artist for an illustrated children's book, and he and the author were working with a very congenial publishing company in Anchorage called Publication Consultants. He arranged for me to bring my manuscript to Evan Swensen for consideration.

Evan did me the courtesy of listening to my explanation of the book and took the manuscript to read and evaluate. A short time later, Evan called me to tell me that he thought it was an excellent book, but it definitely needed polish. Unlike my previous experience, Evan went on to give me practical suggestions, including submitting the manuscript to Edit Ink for a complete evaluation. From that encounter, I learned to punctuate and to spell—apparently my 17 years of post-high-school schooling had been lacking to some degree. I rewrote the book; Evan had me do it again for a final submission, and the book was published. People who actually read *Last Phoenix* have found it a fascinating story and learning experience. Others reject it because it is long.

I submitted a second book to Evan recently which would also be long except that Evan insisted that the autofictional story of my life and career, *Saga of a Neurosurgeon*, needed to be divided into six books. That was done, and the marketing is underway. A third book, *All in Jest*, is in press, and is a shorter novel about the conflicts of the malpractice world that are faced by physicians who undertake the treatment of serious and complicated disease processes.

Separately, I have published two large nonfiction tomes: *On Evolution*, and *Something about Religion*, both too long and too controversial for the style desired by Publications Consultants. Evan has helped me in every way possible to get my books from concept to market and has been most cordial, and willing to discuss the issues of publishing and marketing. He produces a finely constructed book, and has demonstrated sophisticated competence in all aspects of management of a limited market book enterprise. I continue to value him and his expertise.

Fish, Oil, & Follies
Loren B. Flagg

I was named after my great-grandfather, Loren Augustus Flagg. Growing up as a teenager in Southeastern Massachusetts I became quite interested, perhaps fascinated, by the life he had led in the late 1800s and early 1900s. There were a few pictures of deer hunts in Maine, boats he had built, and the East Bridgewater fire department staff where he had served as assistant engineer. There were several old guns he had passed down, including a Civil War era Spencer 56/50-caliber carbine—a gun that had been used by the Union Cavalry, including Custer, at Gettysburg and had helped turn the tide of the battle. There were also several of his old wildlife mounts, including a couple trophy-sized whitetails that had been relegated to the upper hay loft in our early-19th-century New England barn. He had been a carpenter in his early years and many old tools from his trade were still lying around in the barn and a small shop off to the side. Later he became a businessman and eventually purchased a large general store in the center of Elmwood, which he managed, along with becoming postmaster for the village.

All of the above intrigued me, but there was one thing sorely missing. There were no diaries, no notebooks, logs, or any kind of narrative describing my great-grandfather's life. I often thought how sad that this history was lost forever. How neat it would have been to stumble across some narrative of his life to go along with the evidence left behind. And therein lies a big part of the answer to the question of "why" I decided to write my book. My book was basically a memoir centered around my life as a fisherman, fisheries biologist, fishing guide, and fisheries consultant. I thought that perhaps someday my grandchildren, great-grandchildren and maybe even beyond would be interested in what kind of life old great-granddaddy had led!

I had another reason to write a book. There had been two significant historical events in Homer and lower Cook Inlet history involving the oil industry and I had been involved smack in the middle of both. The first occurred in the early to mid 1970s when the state had sold oil leases in Kachemak Bay and then later bought them back. This was an unprecedented action and a very rare victory for citizens fighting against Big Oil. The second event occurred in 1989 when the Exxon Valdez went on the rocks in Prince William Sound and oil from the resulting spill entered Cook Inlet and Kachemak Bay. I wanted to give a first hand account of my experience during these events.

And now for the "how" of writing my fisheries book. It seems that things just fell into place. First of all as a wildlife biology major at Umass I was encouraged early on by one of my professors to maintain a dairy or log of all my field trips. This I did during my career as a fisheries biologist first in Massachusetts, then Florida, and finally Alaska. I extended this practice to hunting and fishing trips, including my guide years on the Kenai River. I also had made a practice of taking photos of friends, coworkers, fisheries projects, scenery, and fish and game harvested during most of my various outings. So when the time came to begin my book I had the resources to draw on to supplement my memory and thus provide a more complete and accurate portrayal of past events.

Getting started seemed to be the hardest part. Inspiration was provided by my wife, Sandra, when upon seeing boredom set in during my first year of full retirement she asked, "Dear, why don't you write a book?" Recalling the Chinese proverb that "a journey of a thousand miles begins with a single step," I decided to apply this philosophy to starting my book. I decided that I wanted to document my experiences and career chronologically so in my mind I could see this project play out chapter by chapter. The first step was to write an introduction; after that chapter 1, then 2, and so forth. As I wrote each chapter I also attempted to locate any photos that would complement that chapter and then label them appropriately. After completing each chapter it might be days, weeks, or even months before I began the next. I would wait for the right combination of time available along with inspiration to begin the next chapter. Once started on a new chapter I typically completed it in a day or two. And so, about a year and a half later I finally completed the book!

Now, what to do next? I got online and researched various methods of publishing and then wrote letters to several publishers. Some wrote back and others were apparently too busy or I was too small fry for them. Some of those writing back wanted a lot of money up front and others sent rather confusing details describing their process. I was examining two of these proposals and also looking into self-publishing when a friend told me about Publication Consultants in Anchorage. I checked out their website and was immediately impressed. Publication Consultants, owned and operated by Evan Swensen, offered five options for the publication of my book. These ranged from Evan's just acting as a consultant to his outright purchase my manuscript. I keyed in on a midlevel option that basically provided a partnership between writer and publisher. My thought was that as a partner the publisher would be motivated to produce the best product possible and then follow up with a good marketing and distribution plan. We would sign a publication agreement and he would then be responsible for the business details that I had little interest in. These included obtaining the copyright, the Library of Congress number, and all the normal business transactions associated with delivering a book to market. Boy, what a relief that I would not have to deal with these issues!

This all sounded good on the Internet and telephone, but I wanted to meet Evan and see if he was someone I could work with. When I did so I came away assured that this was the right way to go for me. Evan was friendly, easy to talk to, and obviously an expert in the business of publishing. He gave me a cost estimate that ultimately proved to be accurate, and we soon signed an agreement. After that there were only a few minor bumps along the road to a finished product. Projects left included final editing, coming up with a title, and finally a book cover design. Then it was off to the printer.

It was an exciting day when the first box of books arrived at our doorstep! First step was to mail a few books off to relatives, close friends, and those individuals who had helped with various parts of the project such as editing, cover design, writing back-cover blips or the foreword. Soon after I was fully engaged in book signings at various locations in Kenai, Soldotna, Homer, Anchorage, and Wasilla. This was followed by attempts to personally market and distribute my book to various smaller stores on the Kenai Peninsula that traditionally carried Alaskana as well as other books by local authors. Some of these stores, including gift shops, would purchase your book outright, while others stocked books on consignment with commissions paid later. This is fine, but takes several follow-up visits to obtain payments and restock shelves when needed.

Final marketing efforts on my part included a mail-out introducing the new book and attending a few craft fairs and Christmas bazaar events. Within the first year I had recovered all costs associated with producing the book and that had been my original goal. And so it goes for the new author! Good luck to all who attempt this rewarding endeavor.

Smarter Than The Alligator
Karen French

Hi, Dr. Karen Lea "Frenchy" French here. I am a teacher, photographer, adventurer, and author! As a child, I always knew I would be an author. I would write my name in beautiful cursive, practicing my author signature.

Upon completion of my PhD, it was time to write my first book: *Dr. Frenchy's Pet Training A-Z*. My mother, for my entire teaching career had always said, "Is your pet trained yet?"

"No." "Well, you have to be smarter than they are!" She was the encourager and impetus for my first book. I wanted to accomplish this for myself and more importantly for her.

"If you want to train your pet alligator . . .You have to be smarter than the alligator." This was page 1, and what a great beginning of this pattern book. I was on my way and now needed a publisher.

I learned of Evan Swensen through an author/teacher friend. I was immediately excited to hire him as my publisher and I have been thrilled at the results. Evan is kind, honest, intelligent, friendly, competent, and patient. I felt I was incredibly fussy in my needs for my book. I wanted everything *just so*. Evan was the best publisher I could ever have hoped to choose. Making the book was the best experience, due to Evan's patient guidance.

I wrote this pattern book to help children learn to read. The thrill of watching children read the book is inspiring to me as an author. I have written three books since, and am happy with each time I have had Evan as my publisher!

In The Footsteps of My Father
Sheldon Gebb

Sheldon Gebb is a first-time author, who has written about the adventures of his father, John Wesley Gebb based on diaries he maintained from age 16 and throughout his lifetime. The idea of publishing a book occurred long after Sheldon discovered the diaries in a suitcase in his mother's home after her death in 1989. Sheldon, the youngest of the four Gebb children, was an admiralty lawyer with an international practice. Sheldon used airport and air-flight time to transcribe all the diaries onto his computer.

Upon his retirement in 2000, Sheldon and his wife Barbara bought an off-road four-by-four RV (license plate HMS TANK) to literally follow his father's footsteps. Over the next decade they explored the places John Wesley Gebb mentioned in his diaries. They started with John Wesley's early years in Jerome, Arizona, his student years at the University of Arizona, and his attempts to strike it rich with a gold mine he developed with friends in the Rincon Mountain range near Tucson, Arizona. Sheldon, during his career, developed a fondness for Alaska while spending considerable time in the Far North representing various clients. Thus, it was natural for them to focus on the diary years of 1908 and 1909 when John Wesley went with three friends to Alaska and the Yukon (Dawson City area) to seek his fortune. The year 1908 was a decade after the original Klondike gold find on Bonanza Creek outside Dawson City and it was the beginning of the era of corporate mining employing huge gold dredges. John Wesley, with his degree in mining engineering, was able to find work with that industry in Dawson City.

Barbara and Sheldon decided to write a book about John Wesley's life and they concluded that the book would have greater interest if it included a description of their travels as they traced the diary entries. In 2000 they covered John Wesley's early life. Beginning in 2001, they traveled to the Yukon and Alaska in HMS TANK, in order to see, to record with photographs, and to research every place John Wesley had mentioned in his diaries.

The Gebbs soon learned that it would require several years of travel to Alaska and the Yukon Territory to adequately research John Wesley's adventures. They relied on archival material from libraries and museums for photographs and information of places long since destroyed. They began their research at the Yukon Archives in Whitehorse, Y.T., where they found extensive historical information about the Dawson City area, particularly of the corporate mining era, which had been preserved. The museum staff was gracious and helpful. Sheldon was able to take digital pictures of photographs showing people and places mentioned in the diaries.

The Gebbs found Whitehorse to be a delightful place to visit. Exploring the city on foot, they recognized some of the sights mentioned in the diary: the prominent cliffs, the Yukon River, a well-preserved sternwheeler, and the vast blue skies. Currently, good restaurants, a variety of interesting stores, and a museum added to the pleasure of being there. After traveling up the Inside Passage to Skagway, Alaska, John Wesley and his friends had traveled by train to Whitehorse and then to the goldfields of Dawson City on the stern-wheeler *Selkirk*. Sheldon and Barbara traveled that route on the Trans Canadian Highway along the Yukon River. They were treated to beautiful vistas of valleys and mountains and the wonderful blue Klondike skies John Wesley had enjoyed. The highway itself was a washboard experience due to frost heaves typical in the Far North. It was worth the bumps. When they arrived in Dawson City they discovered it remained the same as described in the diary. The town is now a Canadian historical site. The wooden sidewalks are built higher than the dirt or mud (depending on the weather) streets. Most of the buildings are historical landmarks that are still in use. They were able to explore the banks of the Yukon River across from Dawson and they marveled at the skeletons of the old riverboats piled in helter-skelter fashion.

Upon their arrival in Dawson City in 2001, Barbara and Sheldon were directed by the locals to the Dawson City Museum. The museum proved to be a gold mine of information. The museum staff were excited about the diaries' firsthand account of John Wesley's employment with the Yukon Consolidated Gold Corporation, referred to as Guggenheim after its owner, and about John Wesley's gold-mining adventures. They provided the Gebbs with a room loaded with notebooks and boxes of historical information. The Gebbs spent several days rummaging through the materials, taking photographs and making notes. Parks Canada personnel provided them with a personal tour of the Guggenheim facilities where John Wesley had worked as a surveyor and as head of the power plant that supplied electricity to the gold dredges.

In 1908 the gold-mining industry in the Yukon was dominated by eastern corporations, which used electrically powered dredges to scoop up tons of embedded river-bottom rock, which contained the prized gold. John and his friends worked all summer for the corporation. Then, in the fall, they decided to strike out on their own and they filed a gold-mining claim for a site east of Dawson City on Slough Creek.

Finding the gold mine site where John Wesley and his friends worked during the winter 1908–1909 was a frustrating experience. Barbara and Sheldon traced the route over which John and his friends had traveled by dogsled in their CJ7 Jeep. It was easy to document the dogsled trek from Dawson City to Slough Creek but locating the mine took several years of exploration. They knew from the diaries that it was on Slough Creek 60 miles from Dawson City near Gravel Lake. They had no idea exactly where it was located, although the diary provided a fairly accurate description of its location. Finally, in 2008 after years of several failed attempts peering through a dense forest of trees and underbrush, Sheldon found a trapper on Gravel Lake who, after reviewing the diary entries, knew exactly where the mine was located! He took the Gebbs on a wild ride through the brush and forest to the mine where evidence of mining was still visible after 100 years.

One of the reasons John Wesley and his friends had chosen the site on Slough Creek was that Alex McDonald, known as "King of the Klondike," had staked a claim there. McDonald had been very helpful and had encouraged them to come to Slough Creek. They were all there, working together when Alex McDonald died at age 54 while chopping wood in weather of minus 50 degree Fahrenheit. The Dawson City Museum contains detailed information about Alex McDonald, which Sheldon was able to use in the book. They discovered he had made (and lost) several fortunes but he was always generous to those who were less fortunate than he.

The Dawson Museum personnel also introduced Barbara and Sheldon to John Gould, a recognized historian of the Klondike gold rush era and author of *Frozen Gold*. John read the diary entries about the mining adventure and discovered that John's uncle, Angus Chisholm, had been one of John Wesley's partners at Slough Creek. Sheldon was able to use the detailed entries John Wesley had entered in his diary to describe the perilous winter of 1908–1909 that his group endured on Slough Creek while digging a mine shaft to a depth of 165 feet. It was the coldest winter recorded in the Dawson area up to that time. Finding no trace of gold, the group abandoned the mine on April Fools' Day, which John Wesley declared to be appropriate. Returning to Dawson City, John Wesley elected to become a bear hunter. His numerous failed attempts provided comical entries for the book. The Gebbs traced his hunting trips by Jeep, marveling at the vast area over which he had traveled.

John Wesley recognized that he had no future in Dawson. His wrangling days in Arizona provided him with enough experience to enable him to hire onto a group of cowboys who were herding horses to the White River for the United States survey team that was surveying the United States–Canada border. By following the diary entries, Barbara and Sheldon were able to retrace John Wesley's journey to the White River. They were amazed to find that much of the area, including settlements, remained just as described in the diary. After delivering the horses John Wesley could find no one willing to undertake a trek across what is now the Wrangell Saint Elias National Park. He thus elected to make the journey solo hoping to find work at the Kennecott Copper Mine. The diary describes a journey fraught with peril. This convinced them to charter a small plane in which they flew over the route John Wesley had taken. They could see that what is now the Wrangell Saint Elias area includes rugged, high, steep glacier-covered mountains with icy streams and rock-strewn cliffs and many waterfalls, an area, the travel books admonish, which is only for the most experienced hiker. Sheldon was able to take pictures of the entire area that had been such a tortuous and dangerous trip for his father. The plane ride was not without its own excitement. In tracing the trip, at one point the plane was enveloped with fog while they were searching for John Wesley's route. The experienced bush pilot, recognizing that the peaks were higher than the plane, retraced his route to clear weather. They were also treated to the sight of a grizzly bear lunging at the plane's wing as they flew close by the mother protecting her three cubs.

Failing to find work at the Kennecott Copper Mine, John Wesley hiked out on a newly constructed train right-of-way and headed for home. That right-of-way is now a dirt road to the Kennecott Copper Mine. The Gebbs drove the old right-of-way to the copper mine area, which is now an interesting national historical site. In addition to exploring the mine facilities being preserved, many tourists go to hike in the ice fields and just to enjoy the magnificent scenery and the interesting historical hotel. The road leading to the Saint Elias National Park facilities is an adventure of potholes and ruts, which Barbara noted in her diary for inclusion in the book. It is worth the trip.

Finally, in 2010 Barbara and Sheldon decided the book was ready for publication. While they were in Anchorage they found Publication Consultants on the Internet and arranged for a meeting with the owner, Evan Swensen. Evan's reaction to their manuscript was swift. He recognized it as an interesting story that lacked focus and was in need of a grammar overhaul. He explained that Sheldon might know how to write legal briefs but that he was an amateur in regard to writing a book. Evan insisted that the book must have a theme and he suggested that we center the story on John Wesley's adventures in the Yukon Territory and Alaska in 1908–09 rather than giving equal treatment to all his life's adventures. Evan introduced Sheldon to a copy editor and writing instructor who would help us edit the book if she thought the story had merit. He cautioned that Sheldon would have to correct everything she marked in red. Evan's evaluation about the editor's reactions was right on point. Fortunately she liked the story.

The draft Sheldon received from the editor was dripping in red ink. Barbara and Sheldon spent the next several months going through numerous drafts learning how to write all over again. Sheldon also contacted the University of Washington, the State of Alaska, the Anchorage Museum and the Yukon Archives to obtain photographs that documented John Wesley's travels. Sheldon discovered that the museums contain a treasure of historical information that can be obtained online.

Finally, in the spring of 2011, Publication Consultants concluded the book was ready to be published. Evan then advised Sheldon that his real work, that of marketing the book, was about to begin. In July 2011 the book was launched at the Dawson City Museum with Sheldon giving a lecture on John Wesley's gold-mining adventures. The Gebbs then traveled to Anchorage to attend book-signing engagements arranged by Publication Consultants. Since then Publication Consultants has also arranged to have the book sold where other good books are sold, and it's now an eBook.

In honor of John Wesley's memory and also in thanks to the people of Dawson City who treated him so well one hundred years ago, all proceeds from the book sales are being donated to the Dawson City Museum for the purpose of computerizing their archives and for other improvements as needed.

We regard our efforts to research archived records and to physically be in and to see every place John Gebb mentioned in his diary of 1908–1909 as the grand adventure of our lives. We are delighted to preserve it all in Sheldon's book thanks to Evan Swensen and Publication Consultants .

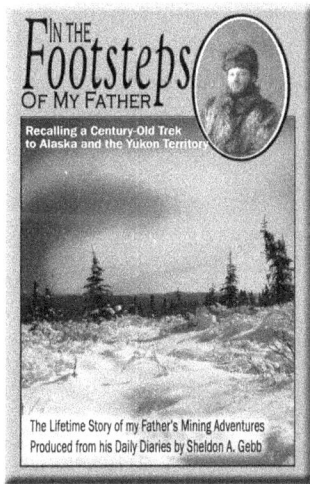

Becoming a Published Author
Cil Gregoire

Writing a novel was on my bucket list in high school, along with moving to Alaska and building a log cabin in the woods. These were big dreams for a Cajun girl still running barefoot in the deep, fertile Louisiana mud. The log cabin in the Alaska woods was quickly achieved, but the completion of a novel remained elusive. It wasn't for lack of life experiences, but rather the consuming abundance of daily adventure that accompanied a lifestyle of commercial fishing in Bristol Bay and Norton Sound in the summer and living remotely in the northern Susitna Valley in the winter. Homeschooling our son, splitting wood, hauling water, baking bread, and inventing a hundred ways to prepare moose were only a few of the items on my daily to-do list.

I did write though, in the form of long descriptive letters to folks far removed from the Alaska experience. These were always highly praised. I also wrote tiny skits for my son and the neighbor's kids, who lived a quarter of a mile away and were also homeschooled, which they had fun acting out. I even started a novel or two…but never finished them. Then after twenty-five years of remote living, we moved to town. Not a very big town, mind you, but "town" by virtue of roads, power grids, and flush toilets. Life suddenly got a lot easier. I joined social outlets like Homemakers and Red Hats, and bought a new computer. I worked for a paycheck during the busy summer tourist season, but began to utilize the dead time of winter by taking up writing. My first endeavor was a skit for Community Theater; my acting troupe, ladies from The Red

Hot Ravens, Talkeetna's Red Hat Society. The first skit was a great success, and I ended up writing five more over the next five years. But I still wanted to write a novel.

"Write about living in the woods," I was told time and time again. Yes, but I didn't want to just write another book about living in the woods. Instead, I wanted to use living-in-the-woods as the vivid, realistic setting for something far greater. And suddenly, thanks to global warming, I also had a great idea for a fantasy/sci-fi, adventure novel. "What if the retreating Susitna Glacier released a magic crystal from a distant world..." and from that thought *Crystalline Aura* was born.

Once I became excited about what I wanted to write, it happened. Of course there were highs and lows along the way, but I never let go, and the work in progress became ever more absorbing of my day-to-day consciousness until two or three years later... or more... I finally reached the end. Rejoining the real world, I suddenly realized I had written a novel! Wow, I did it! Not long after that stunning realization, I came to a daunting brick wall; how do I get my novel published?

Every author, I assume, feels as I do; my story and writing is so great everyone will want to read it. But first people have to know about it. It quickly became evident that I would not be publishing through a large publishing firm. The publishing world was evolving... still is evolving... and one way or another I would publish my novel. I researched options, and without waiting until I could plaster my walls with rejections(I'm too far along in life for that) I found Evan Swensen and Publication Consultants. Evan accepted my work under a plan that I could someway afford, and offered promotional help after publication. In just a few short months after signing a contract, I was a published author. Two years later, with the help of Publication Consultants, I published my second novel, *Anthya's World*.

Selling books is getting increasingly harder. In the short time I have been a published author I have seen the demise of bookstores. Evan has worked tirelessly to find new outlets for authors to do book signings, but we share promotional responsibility. I still truly believe my novels are must reads (If you doubt my words, read my work and see for yourself), and I am working on learning more about getting the word out.

Of course, if you are already famous, selling books is easy. I was doing my initial book release signing at Costco for *Crystalline Aura* shortly after Sarah Palin's book *Going Rogue* came out. My book signing table was set up near a huge stack of her books. I actually did quite well at that book signing, but Sarah Palin did even better, and she wasn't even there!

"My book is better," I told a shopper ignoring my work, but reaching for hers.

"Sure," he said hardly giving me a glance and walked away dropping a copy of Palin's book in his shipping cart. This scenario played out pretty much the same every time I tried it. I can't help but wonder how many of those copies of *Going Rogue* were actually read. Another interesting fact to note, when shoppers bought my book, they didn't buy hers.

Now that I have written two novels, I can see why there has always been a slight distinction between a writer who has written one book, and a writer who has written two or more. I've already noticed that if I can interest the shopper in the series, oftentimes the customer will buy both books. It they only buy one book of the series, I know they will love it so much that eventually they will want the other. There I go, believing in myself again!

People often stop by my table when I'm doing a book signing, not to buy a book, but to tell me about their son, or daughter, or niece, or nephew, etc. who has been working on a book for years and has never finished it. They want advice from me that they can pass on to their af-flicted relative. I did research advice from other writers while trying to complete my first novel and here are a couple of bits of advice that have worked well for me.

First, do not expect to perfect the first chapter of your book before moving on to the next. Your first aim is to lay out a first draft. There is a far greater chance you will finish the work if you at least make it to the end of a first draft. It isn't until you have a first draft and can see your effort in its entirety that you are ready for that magical rewrite and you will have much more insight for the beginning when you reach the end. The perfection will come when you do the rewrite and edit, edit, edit.

Second, don't wait until you have exhausted all your ideas on any giv-en day before breaking away from your work. Stop each writing session while creativity is still warm, keeping threads of ideas you can toy with in your head until you can return to your work. With creative thoughts spinning in your mind, you will be eager to get back to writing. But no strategy will work without consistent effort.

Happy writing!

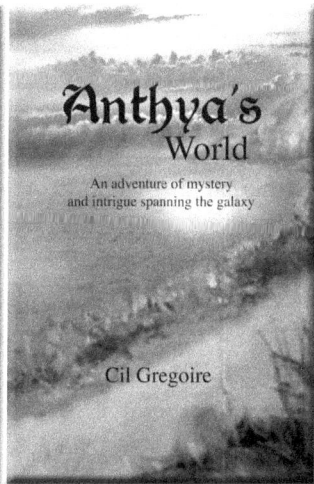

My Frontier Library Beginnings
George Harbeson, Jr.

I have always loved to read, and by extension, to write. Reading and books have been an integral part of the Harbeson family ancestral history for at least a century or more. As a young boy in Wasilla, Alaska, in the mid-1950s, I became an avid patron of the Wasilla Public Library and took full advantage of its small, but diverse collection.

The first summer on our homestead we lived in a long-abandoned military squad tent we'd salvaged from the woods. Wrapped in a mummy bag on a top bunk bed, I spent hours reading in that tent, accompanied by the patter of raindrops on the canvas a foot above my head. I checked out six to eight books every week from the local Wasilla library; books such as the *Hardy Boys*, *Nancy Drew*, *Tom Swift* and Kjelgaard's *Big Red* series, volumes about the American Presidents and other historical figures, books on adventure, exploration, history, science, nature—and all of the science fiction the library had to offer.

Writing is a means of expressing and sharing human experience, and my first fumbling attempts at writing took place in my father's high school English classes. Heroic deeds seemed to be desirable subjects, but alas, I had none to draw from; I hadn't driven a D-8 Cat to the top of Mt. McKinley, nor gone hand-to-hand with a grizzly. "Write about what you know," my father instructed, so I settled for something occupying much of my thoughts at the time–basketball. The result was meager, but a seed had been planted.

Over time, due to my teaching English, journalism, and creative writing, along with my earlier homesteading experiences, I came to see that the seemingly trivial events in my life could encompass deeper meanings and strike a common bond—both humorous and poignant—with other people.

While teaching in rural Alaska I began writing short stories about homesteading, and fiction about life as I saw it in Iñupiaq and Yup'ik villages—each an aspect of a disappearing era in Alaska history. Earning a M.F.A. degree in creative writing at UAA was another consequence of these experiences.

Upon my retirement, those efforts and an interest in small details and family history led me to write a non-fiction book, *Homesteaders in the Headlights*. It is my way to re-live and share my family's history—and a means to offer a perspective of Wasilla and Alaska then, which may serve as a contrast to what they are today.

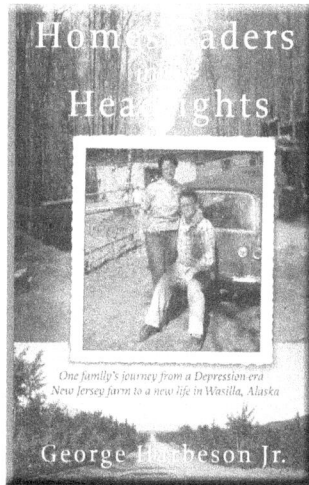

One family's journey from a Depression-era
New Jersey farm to a new life in Wasilla, Alaska

George Harbeson Jr.

Books Written Backwards
How I Brought my Books to Market
Bill Hauser

Introduction

I think I wrote my books backwards. I think most authors get an idea or make a plan that they develop into a story for a book and then find a publisher. I essentially wrote two collections of short stories with no intent to write a story or book. Eventually, however, these did coalesce into books. People ask me, "How long did it take to write?" I always struggle to answer that question because most of the stories were written over a period of about 25 years. The final production required about a year each. Here is how it all happened.

In the beginning

The story of my writing career really got started in the late 1950s in a high school English writing class. Our assignment was to write a creative story. I was a lazy student and it took me a long time to come up with a plan. That resulted in a shortened time to actually execute the plan. Now, remember that this was the age of the typewriter and I could not type so I recruited my cousin to type from my handwritten material. And, being lazy, I did not carefully proofread. You can imagine what ensued. A day or two later, it was time for the critique. And it was my story that served as an example of bad writing. In part, the teacher became confused when "from the light of my match" had been typed as "from the light of my watch." Needless to say, I immediately became humiliated and intimidated with the concept of writing.

Approximately four years later, I was in college and I had put off taking a dreaded, but required, class in English composition as long as I possibly could. Soon, of course, a writing assignment. A day or two later, it was time for the critique. I was nervous and perhaps a bit scared but soon I became astonished. The teacher liked my writing! I was pleased but I assumed it was a fluke. Most of the semester and more assignments were yet to come. My astonishment continued, I did well in the class, and my confidence as a writer grew.

And then

And then came graduate school. This eventually led to writing a Masters thesis in science. The technical writing style is quite different from creative writing. My major professor was an expert scientific writer and a terrific editor. He whipped me into shape and the skills he taught me proved valuable throughout my working life.

And then again

Three important events entered into my writing career. First, I moved to Alaska in 1980 to take a job with the Alaska Department of Fish and Game. This is important because of how it affected my thinking and my writing. Simply speaking, both books I have written are all about Alaska. Alaska experiences and Alaska fishes. I could not have written either book if I had not moved to Alaska. In addition, my job allowed me—no, required me—to travel to different parts of the state and increased my repertoire of experiences in Alaska beyond what I could do on my own or with my family.

Second, during many of these trips and other trips around Alaska, there is waiting time . . . usually because of weather or waiting for some form of transportation such as a boat or an airplane. Most people read books to pass time. Instead, I often would write a letter to share that experience with relatives and friends. These letters simply described the experiences. How I felt. What I saw. How it happened. These were like short stories about the experience and most were written during the activity. They included travels in various parts of the state, family trips, hunting trips, fishing trips, and work activities. I began to realize that many contacts looked forward to receiving the letters and expressed appreciation. On occasion, I was encouraged to publish.

Third, one year, in about the mid 1980s, I had a work assignment to do a stream habitat restoration project. I needed volunteer help and solicited the help from an organization called the Alaska Fly Fishers. They came through, turned out a lot of volunteers, and worked hard for two days to accomplish the tasks. I didn't want to just say thanks and walk away so I contributed an article about fish habitat for their monthly newsletter. One article led to another until after several months, I was invited to commit to write a continuing monthly column and give the column a name. *Fish Talk* was launched and I have been writing Fish Talk ever since.

Fast forward

I retired from Alaska Department of Fish and Game in 2003 and I had a plan for post-retirement. Unfortunately (or, perhaps, fortunately) the plan did not work out quite as I had expected. For several years, I performed several small projects and occasionally wondered about book writing. But one day, while I was home minding my own business, an Alaska radio station hosted an interview and shortly, I realized they were taking about me and my book. After a phone call and a week or so later, I met the interviewee, Evan Swensen, of Publication Consultants. We discussed my ideas and plans and he explained the process, costs, and options.

First, I tackled *Letters from Alaska*. This entailed rereading, sorting, and selecting among the letters I had written and managed to save. Most letters were handwritten. The transcription process was tedious and the sentences needed lots of editorial attention to improve readability while maintaining fidelity to the original writing and message. But all that is boring and I had a bug to do more writing so, for each letter, which became a chapter, I added a large dose of Alaskana that was related to some detail in the chapter. I was feeling good and rolling along until an opportunity to participate in a small research project appeared. Although I enjoyed the research project, one cannot think and write in technical material and non-technical material at the same time so *Letters from Alaska* was put on hold. I kept in touch with Evan and I appreciated his patience.

After I was able to return to the book writing business, I went through the usual process of elation about what I had accomplished and depression about . . . who would care enough to buy a copy. Evan was a constant source of support and encouragement without directing how or what to write. Eventually he guided me through the final process of copy editing, proofreading, inserting images, and printing. Soon I was in a mode of advertising, marketing, and selling.

One more time

Before long, I was thinking more about writing and I thought more about that other favorite topic I like to talk about—fish. I made an outline and discussed the concept with some colleagues and with Evan. Some Fish Talk articles provided a skeletal framework to help get started. The process was actually quite different from the first book. I needed reference material and technical information. I understood the vocabulary and the language after the years of practice with Fish Talk so that part was easy. Some things I thought were facts, however, I needed to correct and I also needed to learn more details about some of the fish I wanted to include. But I enjoyed the learning and relearning all sorts of information about the fish. All facts needed to be checked and rechecked and I recruited colleagues and other experts I had not met for fact checking items in each chapter. The title, *Fishes of the Last Frontier*, went through numerous iterations before this was selected.

The marketing and selling of books is less fun than the creative process of writing and assembling of the material. Some book signings are fun and some are boring. But again, Evan helps out. He has been involved administratively in every step of the entire process and is prompt with sending royalty reports and checks. It is more fun and more interesting to have two books to sell. I am starting to meet people who have already read one or both books and usually the feedback is pleasingly positive. Perhaps the most surprising and satisfying experience in all this was when members of the Alaska Fly Fishers (who routinely read Fish Talk) simply lined up and bought these books without opening the cover. Wow! That was exhilarating and exciting. I also appreciate the satisfied smile of a buyer as I sign a book for them.

After publication, I realized that I had also created a legacy for my family and friends that documents part of my life. And I was proud to deliver my first book to my grandson for his first Christmas. And my second book two years later.

BTW

Evan is fond of reciting, "Books don't sell books. Authors sell books." It gets tiring but he is right on target. It is easy to write a book. And Evan is right. If you want your book to sell, you have to be committed and involved in advertising, marketing, and selling. You are the one who can best describe your book. During signings, I like to put a book on a nearby shelf. Although I may sign and sell some number of books, when I leave, the one on the shelf is still there.

So there you have it. If you have thought about writing a book, decide who is your target audience just do it to it. Writing books backward has worked fine for me.

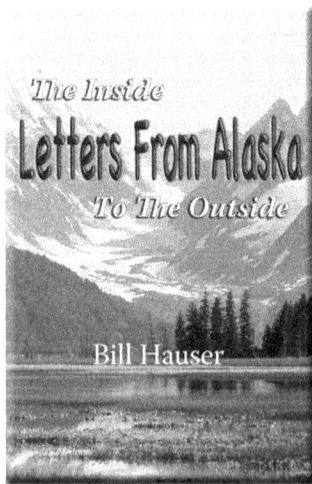

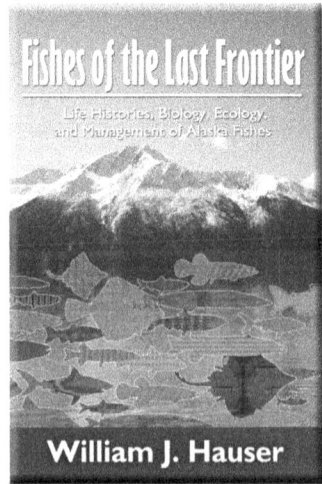

Author of Many Hats
Kayla Hunt

My story began many years ago when I was seven. I hated reading—plain and simple. There were better things to do like climb trees and play in the irrigation ditches. My parents struggled with me for many nights trying to get me to read but all I did was look up and see the outdoors calling me. My first-grade teacher listened to the troubles my parents were having and took the time to find stories equal to the adventures I had on my family's ranch.

I fell into the magical world of literature. I had not realized at that early age that imagination could take me to endless numbers of places. I quickly became known as the girl with her nose in a book.

In fifth grade my passion had grown so much that I found myself wondering if I should start my own book. Why not? The authors I read had done it, how hard could it be? I will not forget the fall day in 1995 when I came home to see an eighty-page spiral-bound green notebook waiting on my bed.

I asked my mother, "What is this for?"

She stated matter-of-factly, "For the book you want to write."

My future was decided right there, with that sixty-eight-cent notebook. I told my mother several months later, and ten pages into my story, "I know what I want to do when I grow up, I'm going to be a writer."

The stories came in waves after I set pen to paper. My imagination didn't stop no matter what I was doing, sitting in class, climbing a tree, running across an alfalfa field or riding the school bus to school. I constantly made up little anecdotes or plots to follow my daily activities. The world of make-believe still continues to run parallel to my life almost two decades later.

Years turned by, one after another, and I had grown up! I became a private music instructor and receptionist. The dream of being a published author had not left my mind. In 2009 I diligently worked to get one of my manuscripts published. Each month I sent out at least ten query letters to publishing houses and agents. I spent any spare moments going to bookstores and researching about the business. Was I prepared for someone to take my baby, only to stretch, delete, and poke it half to death? The only way to find out was more and more research to find exactly what I wanted.

During that same year I decided to move to Alaska. Not long after I arrived, I remember standing in my new bedroom, three thousand miles from everything I had ever known. The New Frontier was where I would make my dreams come true!

One night after I had arrived home from work, I flipped my alarm clock radio on while putting my music and instruments away. An announcement for the Alaska Writers Guild came over the radio and I rushed to a computer. Much to my surprise they were connected to Publication Consultants! Could this company finally give me my fair shot? I summoned up the courage and sent another query letter to Evan Swensen, publisher. I read about the company online over and over while waiting for a response. I loved what they stood for. Could they be too good to be true? I held my breath.

I sat in front of the computer, heart beating, reading the words over and over. Publication Consultants liked my manuscript, found the story interesting, and would be pleased to publish my novel! Had I read that correctly? I read it seven more times to make sure.

I had been right at eleven years old. Writing wasn't hard for me. Now I had to learn how to master the hard part about the publishing world—*Edits*! I took off my writing cap and to really examine the skeleton of my work I needed a few things: a sturdy "editing hard hat," hundreds of hours, a bit of money, and several months of hard work.

November 2010 came and the final pieces were being put together. I had to change like a chameleon again and put on my marketing helmet.

I had to step away from the pages that had been written so passionately and look at this manuscript as if it was someone else's. Criticism is something hard for me to accept, but I had prepared for this step. What would make this story marketable to others? Why would they want to read it? What would make people pick this book up out of the thousands upon thousands published just *this* year?! Titles were perfected, covers creatively designed, and the back cover cleverly crafted, all to spark interest. I found that I loved letting go of some of the control I had over the manuscript and took my publisher's advice. The story was great beforehand, but after I held the final product in my hand I couldn't help but realize it had become spectacular.

One final time I had to change hats and learn to be a top saleswoman. This step has proven to be very hard for several authors. All authors have to find out what works best for them, but the key word is *work*. My new novel could be made of gold but it wouldn't sell without my help. I went back to the books and online articles to find what it took to get my books off the shelf and into people's hands and home.

My story seems so simple and fairytale-like for aspiring authors! It has been a dream come true, yes, but there are not enough pages to fully explain the hours of patience, hard work, and the stubborn willpower to never give up.

To those reading this and wishing their dream rested on white pages—keep the determination to shift through all the "nos" to find a "yes."

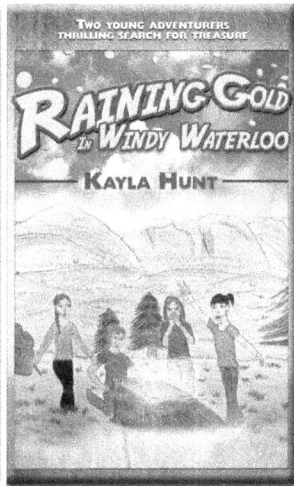

Thrills and Throes
Marthy Johnson

At age four I became a closet writer. It was the only place where mocking siblings didn't find me, and it felt sort of safe. As soon as I learned to read, writing stories—and living them—became my passion, my comfort, and my escape. The characters tended to be everything I was not and would so like to be. In my teenage years I had become quite adept at hiding my writing activities and pretending to be doing homework. Words, sentences, language were always a thrill. The power of them, the heights and depths to which they allowed me to explore the concrete and the abstract gave me a place to go with my feelings and thoughts and ideas, almost to a point where it was scary to pursue them any further for fear I would get lost like a balloon in a wind storm. And so I wrote stories when I could hardly write, and never let anyone read them. Writing is revealing yourself, becoming vulnerable, taking off all the protective layers that keep you safe and whole and protected.

For many years into adulthood much of my writing was just for me— for others just some humor pieces, religious observations, plays, and poetry. My husband kept encouraging me to write for publication, full of hope that it would give me joy, but I froze in fear —one of my deepest regrets, because illness took him many years ahead of what we might have reasonably expected and he never saw his hope realized. It took a long time to understand that no one was the better for my not sharing myself. It was selfish and self-indulgent. If you get hurt a few times— deal with it. You're not the first person who's felt rejection, ridicule, or indifference, and it's not a world-class tragedy. You shake it off, use it if you can, throw it out if you can't.

So I started pursuing the thoughts Ted and I had thrown back and forth, exploring, questioning, and it became a story. In a story there is nearly always someone who is you, the writer, or someone you would like to be. My protagonist was not exactly me. He was male, I am female; he was young, I was—well, a lot older; he was a champion athlete, I was the clumsy kid they argued about having to take on the high school softball team (if they had only played soccer—I can't throw a ball, but I can run and I can kick!). But we asked the same questions and faced similar challenges though different in form. We had to know what was true, and what it meant. Was balance more important than excellence—or could you have both? What makes me who I am, and who, by the way, is that? And is the world really better off knowing the answers to that?

Some writers love only the first writing, that creative burst that culminates in a story that someone might want to read, and that will echo in somebody's soul. I loved it too, but I also rejoiced in the edit, the rewrite. No more worrying about the story line, making it all fit together, flow just right, letting the characters grow and become. That creative part was over. But then the extra treat—playing with paragraphs, finding the winning word and the singing sentence. Looking for the right slant, the passion, the moment my character became all I wanted him or her to be and more, much more. The point where he started doing things I hadn't planned on. Working it and reworking it till I had the words right, as Hemingway said. As right as I could make them at that time and that place in my life, which may not be as good as I will be able to make them next year or ten years from now, but the best today!

I cherished the manuscript for a while. It was perhaps not a literary masterpiece, but it was mine, and it held my thoughts and questions and a few answers and a little of my soul. Could I uncover that for other eyes? And on the practical side—how? Without an agent, knowing full well the chances for a first-time novelist to connect with a big publisher, unwilling to go through the e-publishing channel, and incidentally, without any money to bankroll the publication of my book—what were my options? I had published and regularly updated and sold a desk reference for writers (*Write & Wrong*) some years before, and although it was mostly a self-publishing project, Evan Swensen of Publication Consultants had taken the publication under his promotional wing. I had worked with him for some years as a fierce and fanatic free-lance editor, and knew his integrity. I also knew that from his beginnings in the book publishing business with a little Alaska book he had become a savvy professional with now a publishing company that had left others in Alaska in the dust. And thus it happened. Evan took on *Break Point Down: Game Over*, the story of an athletic champion who seeks to become a man, with the subplot of an abused child who seeks refuge with him and whose agony he doesn't comprehend nor knows how to manage. I pursued his venture into the "real world" and his efforts to translate his superb physical mastery into life skills, spiritually and emotionally empowered so he could somewhere, sometime, somehow uphold someone other than just himself and become whole. I reviewed, rewrote, restructured, rephrased, added and deleted, allowed the characters to make choices I had not foreseen, changed names, and in general tinkered with it till I knew it could bear no more tinkering.

At last it was finished, and it was no longer a manuscript. It had become a book.

A book, however, that needed marketing. And selling. A manuscript is precious, and comforting to hold in your hands, and fun. A book is exhilarating the first time you see it, until, your entrepreneurial innocence torn into shreds, you discover that in today's world there is no safe hiding behind a pen name while the publisher takes care of the book forevermore. The way I'd like to have it, writers write, editors edit, publishers publish, and booksellers sell. It seems like a perfectly natural order of things. They are different and separate activities, though connected. Nothing quite prepared me for the anguish of going out there and actually finding a way to launch this precious newborn, facing demons in the form of potential readers, family members, critics, people who look at the book and never open it, or worse, people who open the book and then put it back. People who pick up your book pretending to go and buy it, and put it down in another aisle. You answer questions such as "What is your book about?" What does she want me to do, tell the whole story so she doesn't have to buy it? "Is it interesting?" Heck no, it's boring as all get-out. "I am going to look at all the other books and then I'm coming back to buy yours." Yeah, right. "I left my wallet in the car—let me run and get it." See ya. "Does it have any pictures?" Well, no. Dr. Seuss is over there in the corner. "I have a stack of books at home that I haven't read yet, but it sounds really interesting." Thanks. I am flattered. "Will you be here next week? I could some back then and buy it." Why not just postdate your check? "You should send it to Barnes and Noble. It would really sell!" A bookstore, why didn't I think of that? Have I made enough money yet to cover the gas?

You have to have a power statement, you are told. A power statement that makes potential buyers salivate and fight over the last copy of your book as you stand there with a benevolent smile, pen in hand to provide your cherished signature. I played with power statements. One for young readers, one for older readers, one for men, one for women, one for left-handed people, one for righties, one for— How much do you tell? Not enough to take the suspense away, if they ever felt any, but not so little that they don't feel the spark. You know how it is with sparks. Some cause an inferno and others fizzle. Most fizzle.

Now for *Write & Wrong* I never needed a power statement. It powerspeaks for itself. Pick it up, read a few sentences, and you know what this book is for. No plot. No suspense. No conflict. No characters. No ambience. It's like a *Chicago Manual of Style for Dummies*. It's about grammar and style and dangling constructions, and it's about the difference between *aggravate* and *irritate*. But *Break Point Down* is different, and you heard it here first: it's much scarier to bare your soul than to discuss the benefits of hyphenating more or less correctly and avoiding double negatives. As an editor, I had worked with many writers, and seen the agony in their faces as they first came to discuss their wounded manuscripts, bloodied, scribbled and squiggled on, and decorated in several colors, which have to do with the continuum of downright absolutely abominably wrong to possibly improvable. I have argued with the already perfect, encouraged the meek, calmed down the hyper, nurtured the timid, bandaged the crushed, and loved and respected writers' work and their courage and their willingness to make it better yet. Some have become bearable, and others very, very good.

So, power statements. Make of them what you will. Pat yourself on the back or apologize for a possibly imperfect piece of prose. Come to think of it, don't. Plan B. Pounce on some scene, some fact, some trait of your book that characterizes the whole story and says enough to elicit interest and not enough to satisfy curiosity. Good luck with that. Most passers-by do not have time or interest to listen to a cutesy commercial. Some have too much time and take all yours, block access by other maybe-buyers, and disclose their most intimate musings on topics of possible interest to them. They rarely buy. Some may argue with you about your power statement, nod earnestly and appreciatively as they cast about for an elegant way to leave, or use it as a bridge to their own soapbox.

The power statement should be provocative but short, informative but veiled enough to arouse curiosity. Don't tell them how it ends. Not too general, not too specific. Not too much, not too little. Don't be pushy, but don't shoo them away from your table. A tablecloth. How many times has Evan told me about tablecloths! At Costco he actually borrowed a fluffy little throw rug for my table. It looked somewhat like a bear cub hide, and I am not fond of animal trophies for decor, but oh well. Another time I called my granddaughter to bring me a tablecloth, and she did—it was the ugliest pea green, and badly clashed with the cover of my book, but it covered the nakedness of my table.

You can decorate the table with items that relate to the content of your book, although that is a questionable technique if that content is not immediately obvious from the cover (and don't get too cute). Although my hero had at one time been a tennis champion, tennis balls are of debatable benefit as come-ons for my novel. The connection with the title is dubious. They do what round things do—they roll, and into awkward places. Crawling on the floor after stray tennis balls does not sell books, unless you are built to provide visual benefit. Besides, it's sort of an after-tennis story, so the balls more or less negate the content. Having no champion-athlete-turned-civilian-looking hunk at my disposal as a prop, I usually just put out business cards and a few bookmarks. I do at times use a banner, often at my own peril, since an innocent hand gesture to emphasize a point in a discussion, or a slight scraping of chairs as you rise to shake hands can bring it down on the head of your unsuspecting once-potential buyer. Banner stands are not remarkably stable.

So you have your books, your tablecloth, and your power statement. Do not look at the guy on the other side of the store surrounded by Harry Potter hordes. It's depressing. Work out your own technique—his probably wouldn't look right on you. If you haven't done this before and you are scared speechless, have a couple of friends drop by to stage a conversation that looks like a fascinating sales negotiation. If you *have* done it before and you are still petrified and your friends have lost patience, look for a person you will probably never see again and strike up a conversation. For me, marketing is easily the most difficult and frustrating part of being a writer. So I said it, black on white. It's hard. It doesn't come naturally to everybody. To some of us, it doesn't come at all. It has to be chased and lassoed and tamed and civilized. The salesman-writer relishes the market and thrives on witty banter with adoring customers. The Business 101 dropout is flummoxed. Flummoxed, I tell you. But never mind, a writer has imagination and knowledge of people and character and the inner workings of the soul, so he can be an actor, and an actor can be anybody, and anybody can be a writer—at least the aforementioned anybody—so . . . ? Writer = actor = salesman. Q.e.d.

Equals may be a bit strong. *Could become* might work. *Will become* for the bold and brazen. But that's the way it works in the 21st century—writers do a lot of the marketing. It is not surprising that as the quantity of writing has gone up with the advent of the word processor and PC, of social networks and texting, the quality has not. Some present-day writers would not have entertained the notion of producing a book had they been born 25 or 50 years earlier, and probably shouldn't have. Others who might not have had the time or the opportunity pre-PC have gone on , with electronic convenience, to write gems. Both extremes are on display: more talent comes out of hiding, and more junk is proliferated. Where does *Break Point Down* fit in? *Buy the book*!

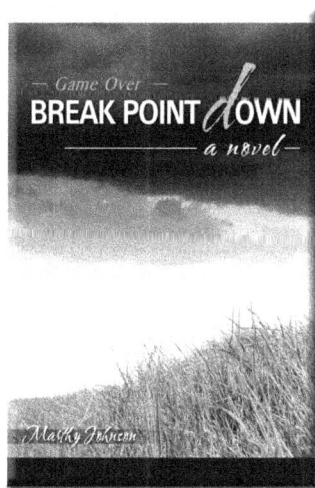

Bringing Carina to Life
Patricia Kilson

I was fourteen years old when I got the most wonderful news. My father had decided to take our family on a sailing trip around the world! He had a midlife crisis but instead of buying a new sportscar or divorcing my mom for a much younger woman, he made a decision that affected our family for the rest of our lives—in a good way.

We sold everything, left our home in Alaska and went to Florida, where we purchased a boat. For the next three years we lived on the sailboat *Carina* and traveled in the Bahamas, Caribbean, through the Panama Canal and up the west coast of Central America, the United States and all the way to Alaska.

After our return to land, we often told of our adventures to family and friends. The time Dad was circled by a shark, or when a whale surfaced right next to the boat, when Cuban prisoners stole my father's watch, or the many times we sailed through raging storms. It was an exciting adventure and all our family and friends kept telling us, "You should write a book." Nobody in my family had any interest in writing a book except me. So I took it on, not realizing how much work would go into writing the story of *Carina*.

I began by taking a writing course at UAA and buying several books on how to write books. I started by deciding to organize the trip chronologically. I created chapter headings for different areas we had sailed through. Then I gathered all the letters we had written to family and friends, many of whom had given us back the letters when we returned. I looked at photos and postcards, my mother's diary and my father's logbook. I pored over maps of the areas we had traveled. I asked my sisters and my parents for their memories and I began to compile hundreds of pages of stories, mostly written out by hand on notepaper. I placed the stories into a notebook behind the chapter headings and thus began my book. That was the easy part.

I felt discouraged because I didn't know how to put it all together. I worked full-time and had two young children to care for. It never seemed like I had any time to sit down and just write. One day, in frustration I decided to take a few days off work and write if it killed me. I made sure I picked days when the kids were in school and my husband was at work. The first morning I woke bright and early and sat down at my keyboard and started telling our story. I continued through that day and into the next. By day three I had at least half my book done and a very sore back from hunching over the computer. It was in a very rough form at that point. I did this again a few times throughout the years; intense two or three days of writing separated by months of inactivity on the book.

Over the next 12 years—yes, I said 12—I continued to write our story. My children grew up and left home! I completed a rough manuscript. I then did fact checking with my father to make sure the locations were correct; after all, I was only a kid when we lived on the boat and I didn't take as much notice of place names as I would now. I had each of my sisters read the manuscript. They remembered some things differently than I and remembered things I had forgotten. I made changes, rearranged stories and the timeline. Then I gathered historical information about the places we had visited and added facts, figures, and information to add to our personal stories.

I had stories I hesitated to put in and agonized over whether or not I should. I left out a few—some were just a little too close for comfort and would lead to more questions about personal issues in our family. Living on a boat together for three years made us a very tightly knit family and I didn't want to explain our family dynamics to those who weren't as close. I did finally put in the story about my attempted rape—I wanted people to know that caution should always be used when out of your own safe places. I was naïve and too trusting. I learned valuable lessons and am much more cautious of people and more aware of my surroundings than I was back then.

Finally I felt like I had a completed book. It was then that I had a proof reader check my first couple of chapters for grammatical errors. It came back with red ink all over it. My heart sank. It took me a few more painful years to go through the manuscript sentence by sentence and word by word. I found that I overused certain words. I was redundant in my sentence structure. Some of the stories were factual but lacked life; I added dialogue. It was a tremendous amount of work. I got teased for years about when my book was going to be finished. Sometimes I would work on it every evening for a week or two and then put it away for months at a time. It was always there though, nagging me to complete it.

When finished I had all of my family read it again, this time specifically looking for errors. It was at this time that my father gave me a harsh critique on certain passages in the book. My feelings were hurt but after careful soul searching, I decided he was wrong and I continued. One must develop a thicker skin when putting family history into a book for total strangers to read. Writing this book gave me a confidence I had previously lacked.

Several years earlier I had heard a radio advertisement about publishing books in the state of Alaska. I was intrigued. I had previously written a few children's stories that I sent outside to numerous publishers, and received nothing but rejection letters. I contacted the advertiser, Publication Consultants, and was quite pleased when the owner scheduled a meeting with me shortly after reading my first children's book manuscript. After Evan Swensen published my first book, *Song of the Raven*, I didn't need to look further for a publisher for the story of my life, *Carina*.

Next came all the decisions about cover design, chapter placement, pictures, font, and general overall look of the book. I argued about a few things but in the end trusted my publisher's judgment. He had published more books than I and was successful at selling them, so I figured he knew what he was talking about—he did. I absolutely love the cover and design of my book!

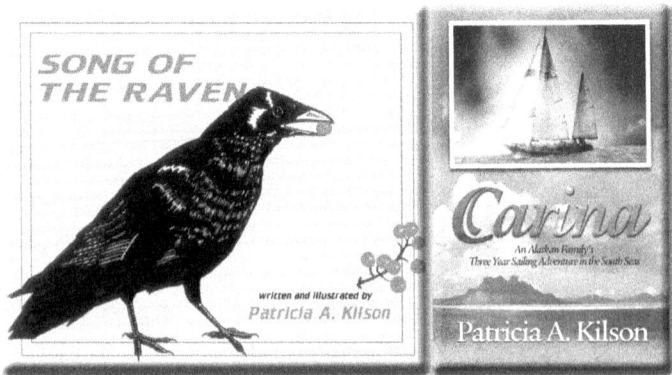

What Possessed Me?
David Kunkle

To me writing a book was something someone else did, someone with patience, imagination and great insight. While growing up, most of these qualities escaped me. My first brush with any type of journalistic endeavor came from the encouragement my mother showed me. Mom thought that taking a writing class at a local California community collage would be just the ticket.

I dropped my writing class after one semester and went back to reading Mad magazine. Actually this class did spark an interest in a higher level of reading choices. Hemingway, Faulkner, Tom Wolf, Jack Kerouac, Hunter Thompson, and others. These authors had such true and deep imaginations. I seemed to gravitate toward the storytellers, the writers of great life experiences, sometimes a great notion. Ah! Yes a story to tell. My first stories came in small ripples, while visiting Europe and Asia. To see first hand the many different cultures, their stories, the people, their glances, telling a life style. These brief encounters weren't enough, not yet anyway, they were adding up to something. What? All would be revealed!

I traveled to many countries and as my many experiences added up I needed to move, so far not much more that letters home to my friends and family. The funny thing was that I wasn't even thinking about writing a book while traveling—not at first. Before I knew it my story presented itself, my partner and I were arrested for smuggling hash into a foreign country. Even then I didn't think about book ideas, just letters home; and sad ones at that. Unknowingly a book had taken seed inside of me. This book grew experience by experience, day by day, month by month, slowly growing in my subconscious, filling me from the inside trying to find its way out—and I didn't even know it.

The next thing I know an opportunity begins, with my seed of experience finding a way to express itself. Now things get interesting, I'm being arrested at the border and ending up in prison in Greece! Upon this incarceration in a Greece court our release was unsure, we went to a total of three appearances, with more time added to our sentences at each appearance, until we were facing twenty-five years of hard time. I was only twenty-three years old so this was a lifetime of hell behind bars staring me in the face. My experiences grew exponentially. Day after day I was met by the new and unknown; how long would this last? I couldn't survive twenty-five years in this "hell hole."

So, would I ever see my friends and family again? My folks were growing older and everyone who mattered to me was ten-thousand miles away. Here I sat in a rundown two-hundred year old prison on an island in the middle of the Mediterranean. *Holy crap*, what did I get myself into? After days, weeks, months it started to sink in, I was going to be here a long while. I seemed to enter a numb stage that was thankfully interrupted by a barrage of letters and packages from home. I began making friends with all the Americans and some of the foreigners. At least there were people to talk to, people who shared my situation. Plans were being made by most of the prisoners conceiving escape; it was on everyone's mind all the time! There seemed to be endless creative ways when it came to taking the "midnight express" over the wall! It consumed some inmates twenty-four, seven, three hundred and sixty-five days a year.

I started again, I would write a few things down, make some plans, tell some stories. What could be? What was? It was my way to express myself, to confirm my existence, I was still here, still alive. So in the depths of this hell I had found a little hope and made it grow! Soon I sort of came to grips with it all, accepting my fate. I was learning the language, how to read music and play the flute. I was bringing my meager life into focus.

I began to forgive myself and take things day to day, meet life head on, on my terms. I would survive all this, I grew stronger inside, maturing again a little at a time. I took responsibility for my actions and tried to stop punishing myself; the Greeks were doing it for me. Finally a little luck and positive thought brought us to a low security work farm at the far end of the island. Now our dreams of escape might just become reality. With so much time on our hands we could make serious plans and change our lives for the better.

Enter, now some serious thoughts concerning the infamous "midnight express!" Right around midnight on a chilly moonless night we launched our fate in a small boat, riding the tide and navigating by the seat of our pants toward freedom. Our lives nearly capsized for good, but with faith and perseverance we survived the worst the sea was offering that night. Toward the conclusion of our seafaring I thought my friend Tom was dead and after a long court room battle I proved my innocence, (or should I say Tom proved my innocence). My friend had resurrected himself just in time to save my l life and my story.

God certainly works in mysterious ways! So after our escape and our eventual return home, we took a little R&R in Amsterdam. I realized that the notion of writing was still very much a nonexistent part of my life. For some reason I knew the spark was still there, somewhere in me. Some forty years passed and I moved to Alaska. My brother was sick and I came to Anchorage to be with him. I felt it may be my last time to spend precious time together. My brother and I were always close. He was my big brother and my best friend. He always had my back and I had his. Donnie passed away three months later. I was with him at the end. I scattered his ashes in a beautiful river on a warm summer day.

The more people I told my story to, the more encouragement I got to write my story, maybe even a book! I would need a publisher and an editor. Once this was solved I began to write and a little over a year later I was finished. Today, my book *Locked up Abroad* is in its second printing. To this day I really have a hard time considering myself an author, I can't type worth a darn. So I end up writing most of my manuscripts the old fashioned way, to pen it! I'll learn to type soon enough, but will I have another book in me? Maybe it will take some kind of new adventure that will enable me to grow another book idea?

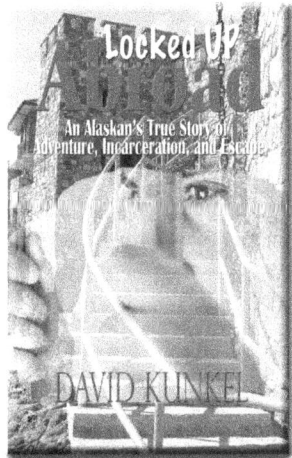

I'm Going to Write a Book
Sharon Lattery

I've always been involved in writing. If it wasn't a diary it was contract and grant work or my journals. I love to read and find authors interesting and amusing. I married a successful writer, author and poet—we've been together 52 years and have critiqued hundreds of books together. One evening after reading a book about an Alaska rural village that lacked a factual basis, I said, "I'm going to write a book." Dennis, my partner, reminded me that there were many steps and tasks that went beyond the mere writing of a book. I ignored him and went into the office and started searching out my journals and a file titled *Humor*.

Various and wondrous positions as a traveling early-education teacher, trainer, and administrator had armed me with a plethora of rural Alaska experiences. It was exciting to think I would finally sit down and begin to put them on paper. If I recall correctly, I wrote two essays that evening—I didn't go to bed until 2:30 a.m. The next day I looked at them and thought I'd better not go on until someone looked at what I had in mind.

I was so fortunate Publication Consultants, a highly recognized Alaska publication business had published my spouse's book *Hunts and Home Fires* and they were helpful throughout the entire process. Evan Swensen, owner of the business, took a look at what I had written and we agreed I had stumbled on a book and should begin writing in earnest. I'm so pleased I selected Evan and Lois. They made me feel special throughout my entire experience.

First, I made an outline of the book and divided it into three parts. My

Life as a Rural Traveler, Growing Up in a Rural Community and final-ly, A Trainer's Clips, Notes, and Anecdotes—episodes that I couldn't write about but that people could probably read between the lines.

Next, I thought I'd better write about me. I had a teacher once who said if your autobiography is more than 300 words and you're not a re-nowned educator or making application for university, keep it short. I did. But the picture next to the section about me in my book says it all!

About this time I realized I needed a large three-ring binder to organize things for me because I shared an office with Dennis, who was also writing poetry and is neat and tidy. By the time I purchased the binder I had the title of my book, *Cold Climate Clips*, and I had gone through hundreds of pictures and was saddened by the fact that I had taken so few.

It was during this time Evan told me to write—that the pictures and the cover and the autobiography all came later. He was so patient with me. I emailed Evan often and he was always prompt in his responses— I'm an early riser and I found he responded quickly.

Okay, I'd write. I had stories, true stories about cheese stored in attics, drunken trainees being sent home from training, favorites that should have been fired, but when it came right down to it I didn't want to write an exposé on my experiences. The positive and the rewarding encoun-ters I had with the rural folks far outweighed any negative memories and I knew in my heart it would be a better book. So I crossed out some of the stories in the outline.

I've never been to an authors' seminar, but I suspect I'd love it. As soon as I write something I want to read it to someone—anyone! Fortunately, I had an audience while I was writing *Cold Climate Clips (CCC)*. Our daugh-ter and son-in-law Stipe had just returned to Alaska and were living with us temporarily. Dennis would listen and comment once in a while, Stipe would always say it was good. Denise was my best critic and would change the grammar. Unfortunately she didn't remove the exclamation marks and when Marthy Johnson, my editor, saw all of them she reprimanded me and reminded me they should really only be used with passionate statements. I jokingly responded that I was very passionate about my writing. I don't recall that she laughed. Anyway, I read every single essay to my family and I believe I even emailed some I especially liked to Evan.

Writers, of course, have different styles, and prefer a variety of environments. For example, my daughter is a writer and she uses earplugs and can write just about anywhere as long as it isn't too bright. Dennis likes quiet and writes late at night when everyone is asleep. I don't care about noise, what time it is, or what is happening—I just write. I'm sure I sometimes annoyed the whole family; while I was immersed in CCC I forgot about everything. Every once in a while I'd holler out "35,000 words!" when I reached a new goal.

My outline was so helpful—I titled my essays and stories prior to writing them and the titles kept me focused. I wish now I had listed more titles. I think the book would have been longer. That is my only disappointment other than the cover. I believe the book would have sold more had it not had an outhouse on the front ….

Something else that sells is a book with lots of pictures. I finally did decide I had enough pictures. And some were excellent pictures that depicted the work that I did and the people I spent a career working with. I also took it upon myself to ask a former colleague for the use of a few of his pictures and gave him more than adequate credit— that was a good move and improved the overall look of the book. I divided all the pictures by chapter and put them in the binder along with the original stories. I did caption each one of them and gave credit to each person who loaned me a photo—this is very important. I believe they should also be listed in the acknowledgement page but that's an author's choice.

After I finished writing and Denise tried to clean it up for me it went to Marthy Johnson, the editor. We met with Marthy. Denise did the final and off it went to Publication Consultants.

Don't think it happened that smoothly—there were a few bumps along the way. People went on vacation. I was sick, and Marthy was backed up with loads of work!

Then comes the time you write the cover description. It sells the book at a glance. I loved writing this part. When I wrote grants I used to have to write short descriptions of projects and give overviews of staff qualifications to meet the criteria for the grant, so this went well for me

The section I had difficulty with was the acknowledgements. I had so much help and so many friends who encouraged me and was so appreciative of Evan Swensen at Publication Consultants for offering me the plan as a way to publish my book.

Finally, the day came that we sat down and put the pictures with the printed page. I was finished. Evan said I had one more chance to look at it before it went to the printer.

He would have to send it to me because we were off to our cabin in Seldovia. It came and there were a few changes—off it went and when we returned to Anchorage for supplies I picked up my new book. Until you publish you'll never know the feeling you have in your stomach and head when you first hold your book. It's amazing!

Next, we scheduled book signings. We served candies and juice at one because of the size of the facility. We had an open buffet at the second because it was large and accommodated a large number of folks and we didn't serve anything at the third because it was so crowded. Book signings are a good idea! If you don't get out and sell your book it doesn't sell.

I was excited throughout every step of building my book. The creative processes were remarkable and the mechanics were positive learning experiences made possible by the people who guided and helped me through the process.

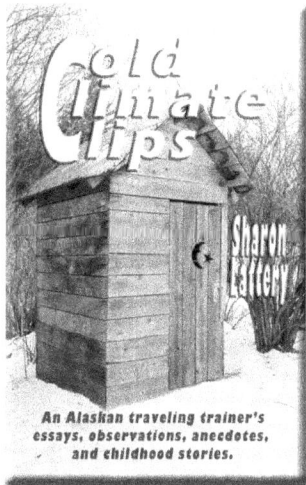

An Alaskan traveling trainer's essays, observations, anecdotes, and childhood stories.

The Hardest Job You Ever Love
Steven C. Levi

Perhaps the most important thing to say about writing is that if you don't love it, don't start. It is a long and lonely road and you are not going to die a millionaire. But it will be the hardest job you will ever love.

Getting published is really a three-step process with the first one being the hardest. That first step is to have something to say. While this may seem obvious, a lot of writers seem to have missed that first step. Now, admittedly, sometimes it is on purpose. If you want to sell a mystery novel you'd better have a murder as close to the front of the book as possible. But then again, if you want to write *genre* all you have to do is know how to type. Quality books start with quality ideas. Personally, I believe that if I do not have something new or different to say I'm wasting my time as a writer. And I'm doing more than wasting the readers' time. I'm discouraging them from looking at my other books. I want readers to know that every book I write is different from every other book on the market—and different from the last one of my books that they read.

As an example, my mysteries are impossible crimes. These are crimes where you cannot figure out how the bad guys did what they did. This gives my novels an extra dimension. Not only does the detective have to solve the crime, he has to do it while he is figuring out how the impossible crime occurred in the first place. In *Heinz Noonan and the Empty Aircraft* a plane leaves Seattle with 245 passengers and a crew of 12. When the plane lands in Anchorage it is empty–and the bad guys want $25 million in precious stones for the release of the passengers and crew. Now the detective has to deal with the payoff, figure out how 257 people can vanish into thin air and, at the same time, stop the bad guys from getting away with it.

The second part of the writing process is the most fun: the first draft. That's the l-o-n-g moment of discovery. You will get into the book and it will begin to write itself. If you are working on a novel, the characters will generate their own conversations and while you may believe you have a plot line, don't count on following it. Follow where your characters lead. The same is true in nonfiction except that you are following facts. I have yet to do a nonfiction book where I knew when I started where I was going to end up. I went where the facts led.

The last part of the writing process is what I call "the grind." You have to edit and revise, edit and revise, edit and revise, edit and revise, edit and revise until you are sick to death of the book. You put it aside and, a few months later, you edit and revise, revise and edit, and edit and revise. Then, when you are so sick of the characters you cannot see straight, you start to look for a publisher.

I have been writing since the 1960s and in the decades since then I have watched in horror as the writing industry died, came back to life, died again, and came back to life only to die and come back anew. Up until the 1980s the publishing industry was dominated by about a dozen publishers and every town in America had scads of bookstores. By the early 1990s this condition had reversed itself. There were hundreds of publishers and most towns in America had one or two bookstores. Then, with the rise of the personal computer, *anyone* could write and a lot of anyones did. The belief was that if you had a word processor you were a writer. Overnight secretaries became technical writers and the professionals in the business disappeared. The quality of proposals, annual reports, newspaper stories, speeches, and other forms of communication went way down. Email and now texting continue this downward trend. Then came e-publishing and the quality of writing went into the sewer. At the same time, the *big money* in writing disappeared. That was the novel-to-screenplay cash. At the same time, movies became more expensive to make and with so many cable channels the made-for-TV market disappeared entirely. Hollywood dispensed with original movies and produced knock-offs. When was the last time you saw an original concept on the screen?

However, and this is a very big *however*, writing is making a very strong comeback. It is making that comeback not because writing is getting better but because writers and publishers–ink-and-paper as well as electronic–now understand that to be profitable they actually have to market their wares.

In the old days the publisher took care of the publicity. Those days are gone forever. Advertising is expensive and the competition is ferocious. Unless the author has a big name a publisher cannot afford to print the book, distribute the book, advertise the book and still make the big bucks. On the flip side of the publishing coin, you can upload an eBook for free but there are millions of eBooks out there and to make a dime you have to market, market, market. That's not a dollar-and cents task; it's a time task.

Now the emphasis is on getting your name *and* the book out. That's why publishers like Publication Consultants are so important. Not only will they get the book out–yes, it is expensive–but you make your money back because if you don't make money Publication Consultants doesn't either. That's why you should take advantage of every book signing you can. It sells your book—which makes Publication Consultants happy—and it publicizes your writing. The marketing you do today is going to sell your books for the next decade. I like dealing with Publication Consultants because I get an email every month telling me how many books I did–or did not–sell. I have books with other publishers and have never received a statement.

Perhaps the most important thing to say to a writer is to lose your ego. If you are writing the story of your life because you think it's been so interesting—don't. The worst books I have ever read were written by people who had interesting lives but didn't know how to write. They are ego-driven and their books end up unreadable. That's too bad because a lot of very interesting people are going to have their life's story disappear from history.

To finish on a personal note, one of the strongest incentives to being a writer is that you have a creative life. Once you are hooked on creativity you are not going to have any downtime. I think of plot lines as I am driving to the store. I read an interesting tidbit in a magazine and see if I can twist it around enough to use it in a short story without someone saying "Hey, I saw that in an article in *Newsweek*." I have stolen every great line any of my friends have ever said. I have ideas for books I will never write and have been personally shocked at the high quality of books that came from concepts I thought were mediocre at the time. Life is full of surprises and, as a writer, you are going to get a lot of them. At the very least you will not spend your twilight years sitting on a rocking chair on the front porch thinking about nothing.

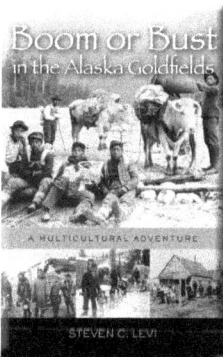

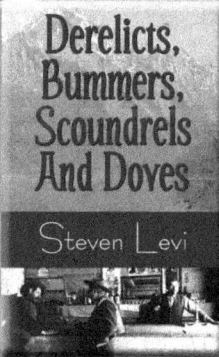

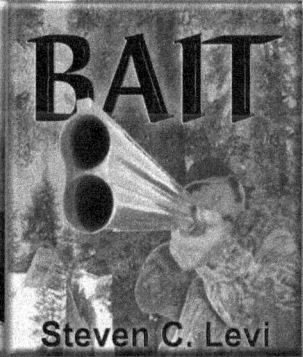

Aviation Fascination
Gregory P. Liefer

The path to becoming a successful author can be a time-consuming and numbing process, often filled with a strong dose of rejection, indifference, and even self-doubt. That's not to say a new author can't find success through a large, national publisher or even a regional one, but statistics show that is rarely the case. Read the biographies on many of today's well-known authors and you'll find they struggled for years before becoming recognized best sellers in their respective fields. With that said, don't be discouraged. No one knows your writing better than you. If you believe in yourself and are convinced you have the "right stuff," be persistent and do what it takes to make your book a success.

Notice I emphasize *successful* author, as opposed to *published* author. Some authors are satisfied with only seeing their book available at the local bookstore or as gifts for family and friends. If that's your goal, great—the road is much easier. There is a bounty of self-publishing and print-on-demand companies more than willing to place your work in print, no matter the content or quality—all for a price, of course. But if your goal is fixed on a higher plateau, if you have the idea, the story, the talent, and the determination, I believe you can and will succeed.

My journey to becoming a successful author, and I use the word *successful* reluctantly, is a long one, encompassing more than 20 years and two works each of fiction and nonfiction. The two fiction works were never published, the two nonfiction works were. Both nonfiction works reached marginal success in the geographical region where the material was focused. One made a good sum of money for the publisher and very little for me. The other has and continues to make money for both of us.

When I first had the idea of writing a book I was a United States Army warrant officer stationed in Germany, living an enviable lifestyle of flying on an almost daily basis and married to the woman of my dreams. In my late twenties at that point, I was already living a lifelong goal of being a pilot and serving my country. One of my many hobbies was reading, a carryover from my childhood that remains today. Unintended, it was a propensity for reading that eventually led to a slow progression into writing.

Of course, as an adolescent and into my adulthood I had brief thoughts of becoming a writer, but never seriously, always dismissing them as unattainable. Other pursuits in life were by then far more important. That changed after reading a particular novel purchased from the post exchange bookstore, whose title has long been forgotten. The plot was terrible, outdone by even worse writing that I struggled to get through without throwing it in the garbage. But finish it I did, and with the realization that if a book of such low quality could be published and make money for the author, then surely I could write something that would be far better.

Thus began my fledgling writing career. The next day I was outlining a great story, which from my perspective contained all the elements of a best seller: an enthralling plot, adventurous characters, and political intrigue. I wrote in my spare hours over the next three and a half years, finding the time after long days at work, military relocations, the birth of our daughter, and a litany of typical family and career commitments. Eventually the story was transformed into a working manuscript, and with the loving assistance of my wife, was edited, altered, and rewritten several times until I was satisfied. But the endeavor was far from complete, for then began an unknown and sometimes harder process of finding a publisher.

I soon learned from dozens of rejected query letters and the informative purchase of a current *Writers Market* at the local bookstore that my previous endeavors had been mostly a waste of time. Anyone seriously thinking of finding a publisher for their manuscript should purchase a current copy of *Writers Market* and/or *Literary Market Place*. The books provided valuable insight on how to prepare your manuscript, write query letters, find agents or publishers that pertain to your genre, and a host of other insightful information.

Because I was still convinced my manuscript had national marketability, I began a second phase of finding a literary agent to represent my interests with major publishers. Note that almost all major publishing houses will not accept a manuscript unless submitted through a literary agent. Regional and smaller publishers are different in that they will often accept manuscripts directly from the author. Another value of *Writers Market* and *Literary Market Place* is that they contain detailed lists and rankings of all publishers and literary agents in the United States and Canada. *Guide to Literary Agents* is also a useful publication.

After a few months of more query letters, summaries, and sample chapter submissions, I found a literary agent willing to accept my manuscript, signed a contract, and sat back waiting for the inevitable fame. I was naïve, of course, and a year later, with the agent contract expired and a pile of rejections from numerous publishers, the agent bowed out, citing the decline in the economy and less than enthusiastic comments from some of the editors. The truth was I had a good story, but my writing was very rough and amateurish.

I rewrote the manuscript again, intending to achieve a much better product. Unfortunately, with my new insight, the process didn't develop into anything near what I thought it should. I finally admitted to myself that my writing was as bad, if not worse than the novel which inspired me to begin writing in the first place.

During the next several years my writing was placed on hold as I concentrated on family and my military career, until a medical condition provided the leisure time for more writing. I began with a short story that eventually transformed into a 400-page manuscript. The transformation was not immediate by any means. In fact, the transformation continues today.

Eventually the second fiction manuscript was completed, or so I thought, and I began another quest to find an agent and eventual publisher. The rejections were quicker and harsher this time, which was actually welcome. Finally I was receiving some honest critiques on my writing deficiencies and, even more valuable, suggestions from editors on how to improve. It was a whole new awakening. My stories were interesting. I only needed the developed writing skills to reach a level of marketability.

While my second attempt at a novel was advancing, I began researching aviation accidents and fatalities in Alaska, more as a hobby than with any intent to write nonfiction accounts of the tragedies. The inspiration for the research was curiosity over the numerous crash sites I encountered during my extensive flying career in Alaska. One investigation led to another, often while discovering references to other previously unknown accidents, until unintentionally, volumes of information filled several filing cabinets.

At that point the realization of the historical significance of the material was obvious. Far too many of the stories were never explained in any detail, yet were captivating accounts of adventure, mystery, survival, and heartache, often as interesting as any novel. Together, the stories were a chronology of aviation history. Putting it all together was the challenge.

As my writing focused on nonfiction, I penned the aviation tragedies to paper in a collection of individual stories. First came *Broken Wings: Tragedy and Disaster in Alaska Civil Aviation* in 2003, followed by *Aviation Mysteries of the North* in 2011. *Broken Wings* has done well and is in its second printing. *Aviation Mysteries of the North* has done equally well and is also currently in its second printing, yet there is a significant difference between their successes.

In my haste to have *Broken Wings* published, I signed a very one-sided contract with a less than trustworthy publisher. The limited royalties I've received are almost laughable, yet the publisher has done very well at my expense and has failed to honor major provisions of the contract. Make sure you do your research on what should and shouldn't be in a publishing contract, and on agents and/or publishers who are intended business associates. I didn't and nine years later I'm still paying the consequences. The *Writers Market* and *Literary Market Place* will again be of great assistance. An informative website is *Predators and Editors* at http://pred-ed.com/.

When dealing with a publisher, or any business for that matter, don't accept assurances over the phone or in person. Anything important enough to discuss should be in writing. Clarify everything you feel is essential. Some things are negotiable, some are not, but make sure it's on paper.

I also suggest being careful of using a Canadian or other foreign publisher. If future legal issues do somehow develop, you'll more than likely have to litigate through that country's legal system. Although a remote possibility with a reputable publisher, it can be an issue with less honest ones. By doing your homework before selecting a publisher and before signing a contract, you will gain information that will hopefully alleviate any future problems.

Soon after finishing *Broken Wings* I began researching and writing my second nonfiction book, *Aviation Mysteries of the North*. By this time I was retired from the military and employed as a contract helicopter pilot on the Trans-Alaska pipeline. A set schedule of equal work and off-duty time allowed more writing opportunities, ending with the manuscript being completed in a shorter time span. Well illustrated and better written, I was certain the book would be a success.

Unfortunately, I made the same mistake with *Aviation Mysteries of the North* as I had with *Broken Wings*. Only after I signed the contract did serious problems with the first book, *Broken Wings,* begin developing, and I knew I was in for the same trouble with *Aviation Mysteries of the North*. Luckily for me, the publisher missed the two-year publication date, and after some legal intervention I was on my own again.

While this was transpiring I continued working on the second novel, never completely satisfied with the result and always adding or changing as my writing skills matured. Let me add that my changes became almost an addiction, focusing too much on the grammar and not nearly enough on the flow or readability of the content. For me, I've found stepping away for a few days or even weeks can place a whole new perspective on your writing, providing a fresh and more honest assessment.

Obtaining a sincere assessment of your work is another important consideration. Family and friends often have a false, oversupportive view of your writing, or hide their views, being reluctant to provide negative comments. Find a good editor and unbiased readers so you can receive honest critiques. Negative comments are equally important, if not more so, than positive ones.

While writing continued on my second novel and the contract expiration for *Aviation Mysteries of the North* was being argued, I added new information and more photo images as they became available. Research continued and several of the stories were rewritten. Even better this time, *Aviation Mysteries of the North* was ready for a new publisher.

Finding a new publisher, unfortunately, wasn't any easier than it had been before. There were plenty of publishers willing to accept the book, most with outrageous contracts which provided them lifetime rights, my investment money, and limited profit potential. Literary agents necessary for national publication weren't interested, claiming the material was only marketable in a small regional market. I still went through the process, trying again and again, without success. After months of frustration, self-publishing appeared to be a viable alternative.

Once a manuscript is submitted for copyright through the US Copyright Office, which is strongly recommended, self-publishing advertisements will begin inundating your mailbox and e-mail server. All will have exorbitant claims for your future success. Be wary. Most will provide accolades on anything submitted, regardless of the quality. With your money they will design and print the books for you. The rest is up to you. Distribution, advertising, and sales are your responsibility. Depending on your business expertise, knowledge of the publishing industry and quality of the material, you might make a profit, or more likely, have a garage filled with cases of unsold books, and wonder what happened.

If you have any inclination toward self-publishing, I strongly suggest *The Complete Guide to Self-Publishing* by Ross and Ross. The information can be overwhelming, but whether you pursue that avenue or not, the content is very useful. It certainly swayed my decision to use another alternative.

Publication Consultants, a smaller but well-respected publisher had been on my radar for some time. They had a good reputation and for *Aviation Mysteries of the North's* anticipated market, were a proven successful Alaska publisher. Even so, after dealing with other regional publishers I was skeptical. Only after speaking with the owner, Evan Swensen, on several occasions and reviewing his company's different contract options, were my concerns alleviated. Since I was confident in my book's future sales and profits, I chose a contract requiring my own investment. I paid for the process of editing, design, layout, and printing, with Publication Consultants handling the distribution and shipping. Because of that, my profits have been substantially higher than if I had chosen a more conventional contract.

To put it in perspective, *Aviation Mysteries of the North* has resulted in twice the profits, with half the number of books, in a quarter of the time of *Broken Wings: Tragedy and Disaster in Alaska Civil Aviation*. Having the right publisher and the right contract makes all the difference in the world.

Being a published author doesn't mean success is a given once the book is in print. Sales will in large part depend on your own marketing and advertising. Although Publication Consultants has the contacts and means of distributing your book, getting the book on display for potential buyers is often contingent on your direct involvement. Book signings, literary reviews, newspaper and magazine reviews, news releases, and contacting potential retail sources are absolutely necessary if you want to be successful.

Research your book's potential market and use it to your advantage. As an example, the content and historical perspective in *Aviation Mysteries of the North* provides interesting information to visitors of aviation museums and libraries, particularly in Alaska and Canada. By contacting the museums and libraries directly I've generated curiosity about the book, resulting in orders that would not otherwise have been available. The same is true for reviews. Sparking attention from retailers and readers can and will result in sales. Advertising is a positive influence on sales; the more the better.

Currently I'm involved in two writing projects. My attempt at a second novel, hopefully my first to be published, is ongoing. I'm still my harshest critic and will continue editing, rewriting, and changing until I'm satisfied the manuscript is complete. I anticipate a release in 2013. A third nonfiction book on aviation history is also in the works, entailing more disasters and mysteries.

Still an avid reader, I not only wrap myself in the authors' stories, I study their style, their plot twists and developments, their characters, descriptions, and dialogue—everything that makes their stories what they are. Maybe I'll reach that level, maybe not, but the process continues.

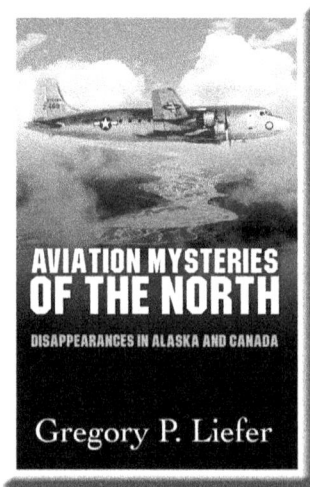

AVIATION MYSTERIES
OF THE NORTH
DISAPPEARANCES IN ALASKA AND CANADA

Gregory P. Liefer

A Shared Journey
Christy Lowry

Just days after losing our eighth-grade daughter in a sudden, tragic auto-pedestrian accident on her first day of school, I knew beyond any doubt that I would write a book chronicling what happened and how God restored us—in short, our story—and that someone not then revealed to me would publish it. Just days after losing our daughter, I began a grief journal that grew to more than 1,000 pages that first year. Every impression, hope, dream, helpful mentoring or healing tool I came across (or which came to me) went into it. Many early morning hours my fingers clattered away on the stiff, resistant keys of an ancient typewriter, whose noisy clicking kept my patient husband awake in our nearby bedroom. Those were the precomputer days when correcting typos became its own (ongoing!) project—no immediate and automatic keystroke corrections rescued us back then! But conviction and a driving need to get my thoughts and feelings down on paper drove me on.

Little did I know how this emerging journal would provide me the depth and detail I needed to write both *PAM, Life beyond Death: Joy beyond Grief*—and its sequel, *Hope Renewed: Picking Up the Pieces after Loss.* While loosely scattered thoughts at first predominated in its early pages as I wrote, my brain amazingly and spontaneously picked up the pace, organizing and correlating details as I went; and I was increasingly able to pinpoint and identify practical nuts-and-bolts healing and mentoring helps. At the same time, I was amazed and encouraged to see my healing progress visually taking form on paper; it gave me a progressive overview I wouldn't otherwise have had, and gave me an exponential uplift emotionally.

Little, too, did I know the preparatory role my journal would play in defining for me what a writer is and why we write, targeting my audience, and ultimately providing both my focus and baseline upon which to structure and organize my books. More than I realized at the time, journaling put all the information I needed in one place, pinpointing key points, experiences, and relevant scriptures. What an invaluable tool!

But much work yet lay ahead. I still had to refine my focus and organize all this information into a coherent manuscript worth publishing and reading. Early brainstorming interviews with friends and family members (some taped, some not) helped me here.

As a then inexperienced writer, accomplishing it was a bigger challenge with *PAM*; I had to first learn the ropes from the ground up. How to condense so much material, with seemingly endless pursuable options? What material added to, or obscured, our story? What to include or delete? How to reign in my persistent tendency to write above my readers on a doctoral thesis level? How long should the book be? Should there be a sequel? Or several sequels to cover what a slim 96-page copy of *PAM* couldn't? Resolving these issues meant endless—and I mean endless—writes and rewrites, paying relentless attention to grammar, syntax, spelling, my typos and new ones that slipped in with each rewrite, whether mine or someone else's. This is the first stage where one finds out whether or not one has the necessary drive, determination, and self-discipline to continue.

But all this rewriting had its silver lining. With each new draft, I could see my organization improving, greater clarity of expression emerging—making each following rewrite that much easier and faster to do. Seeing *PAM* thus take shape through this process exhilarated me, vindicating my determination to persevere.

Well, the day came when I felt my manuscript was ready for the next level: securing a publisher. How would I do that? Although I had no idea, I intended to find out and quickly—I wanted my message to get out and reach as many people as soon as possible.

I began my publisher search by culling the brains of everyone I knew. Two close friends recommended the same publishing house: Publication Consultants, headed up by Evan Swensen. Their not knowing each other put them in the valuable category of independent recommendations, motivating me to meet and interview their recommendation.

The day of the interview came. Would my potential publisher understand and appreciate my goal: to share our God-given inspirational journey of comfort and hope with other hurting grievers? Would he consider my manuscript, already the product of numerous rough drafts, publisher-worthy? Would our personalities mesh well enough to work together? Would my book (and its sequel, *Hope Renewed*) fit in with his/her interests, goals for his company, style?

The Interview went well. Evan patiently answered my barrage of questions although he later allowed as how my blitz of questions took the cake. But I had heard some horror stories about other publishers, had a limited amount of money to invest in this project, and knew the wrong publisher could take advantage of my inexperience.

What followed next was a series of meetings with Evan that covered not only publication costs and book pricing, but such key details as what kind and thickness of paper stock, choosing readable fonts, photos (black and white, or color?). We also looked ahead to marketing strategies for getting *PAM* into stores, churches, libraries, schools alongside Evan's own many, and growing number of public events. All of this would help me network and expand my outreach down the road.

The whole process fascinated me, and I appreciated Evan's ample opportunities to participate, i.e., choosing the title and book cover. Many publishing houses arbitrarily make those decisions.

And of course, one book often leads to another; realizing so much was left unsaid in *PAM*, I wrote and published a second book alluded to earlier: *Hope Renewed: Picking Up the Pieces after Loss.* Building on my experience with *PAM*, I supplemented my journal with interviews with my customers. After my frequent in-depth conversations with them, I'd dash to my table and note down highlights, earmarking them for future use before I forgot them.

Hope Renewed progressed much faster due to several factors: I was now an experienced published author with my own supportive publisher; so I didn't have to shop for a publisher, itself often a time-consuming process. Plus, I wasn't multitasking with other projects (while writing *PAM*, I had been simultaneously absorbed in a five-subdivision effort to obtain a neighborhood park just two blocks from our home.).

Additionally, I had baseline contacts in place due to earlier networking efforts. These contacts in turn provided me with second-, third-, (and more) generation contacts. I not only enjoyed networking, it personalized my book-writing efforts for both the other parties and me. In short, I made long-lasting friendships in the industry.

Right after *PAM* came out, I plunged into book signings, some arranged by, and participated in with Publication Consultants, others arranged by me. This approach expanded my outreach to the public; and I discovered just how much I enjoy book signings. I learn as much from the customers as they do from me. They share their own interesting stories and insights, and are the best opportunity to meet, greet, and share with the public. I'm unconventional in that I circulate among shoppers entering and leaving the store (versus sitting at my table), seeking to connect with and engage them. Even though our economy has made sales more challenging, you never know who will remember your book(s) and purchase later. At any rate, it's the industrious, committed, and enthusiastic author who sells books.

Other, at the time seemingly unrelated events can also rebound to one's favor in the marketing arena, extending interest as well as introducing new people to one's story. In our case, periodic coverage by the *Anchorage Daily News* on the progress of the emerging Pamela Joy Lowry Memorial Park (and beyond) has contributed to a tangible, enduring, and continuing neighborhood interest in, and commitment to our story. Local residents have helped the Department of Parks and Recreation maintain and refurbish the park over the years. Visitors have spoken of "going to Pamela Joy" as if visiting the essence of her presence," and Dave Stroh (KTVA Channel 11) did a touching 25th-anniversary feature about it and our daughter.

What was my highlight experience in writing *PAM*? And *Hope Renewed*, too, for that matter? Holding *PAM's* first published, tangible copy in my hands, ecstatic gratitude combined with surrealistic disbelief surged through me. With God's help, we had made it! I felt touched beyond words. Now we could go out and positively touch other lives, by first chronicling our family's spiritual journey in *PAM*, then passing on the torch of comfort and help to other hurting grievers (and their comforters) in *Hope Renewed*, whose practical everyday healing helps cover all situations. In short, we could now reach whoever needs and wants help and encouragement, regardless of age or circumstance. Thus, I felt a solid sense of accomplishment upon completing and getting *Hope Renewed* published.

Finding Publication Consultants, and their subsequent willingness to publish both books, I truly feel was a God thing. Especially since their company has continued its exponential growth by taking advantage of every available technological advance and pursuing every available opportunity when not creating their own—they're not the largest publisher in Alaska for nothing. They know the necessity for, and benefits of, hard work and persistence—and see and appreciate it in others. And if there are questions, even repeats, this family-owned company steps up with the answers, in keeping with their stated goal of helping people publish the book each person has within.

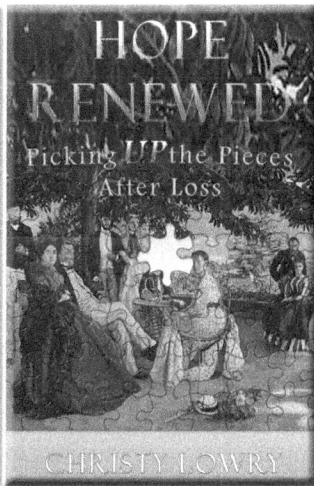

Nice Niche
Bonnye Matthews

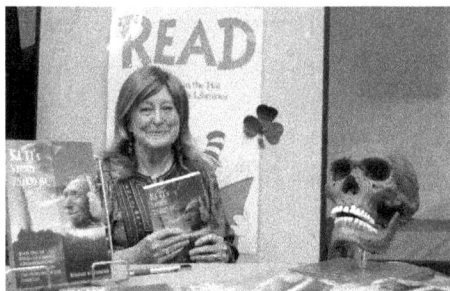

In 1974 a trip to Anchorage to teach an instructor's training class made me realize that I wanted to live in Alaska. It took me until 2005 to realize that dream. An avid researcher, I began to search for the roots of the first people of the Americas, expecting those roots to be Alaskan. It took little time in the books and periodicals at the library to discover that there is an archaeological issue as to who, when, and where those people took root in the Americas. Years of research made the issue clear. There is the Clovis First view (no one in the Americas prior to 12,000 years ago) and the Pre-Clovis view (people in the Americas as far back as 20,000 to more than a million years ago). About the same time research showed that Neanderthals, a people typified as ape-like, stooped over, incapable of speech as we know it—a word used to cast aspersions on others when their intelligence is called into question—those Neanderthals were quite bright and as capable as we, only without the technology. Those same Neanderthals were light skinned, blue-eyed, red-haired. I discovered that we carry Neanderthal DNA. I was hooked on the issue and early man and chose to speculate, carving out an unoccupied niche for my work, a novel series on the Pre-Clovis peopling of the Americas. Non-fiction was already taken—by the experts.

I was born in Richmond, Virginia, where I taught English. My favorite childhood memories were in Georgia when my military family lived at Hunter AFB. Available to young people next to base housing was a great pine forest where opportunities to play abounded. Often alone in the forest I learned to be acutely aware of surroundings: to see the slightest movement, to smell snakes and lizards, to hear the slightest sound, to walk soundlessly. I wondered about previous times in the places where I walked, asking questions such as what was it like a thousand or more years ago—even further back? I imagined those times.

My "grown up" years consisted of teaching and doing personnel work (personnel management evaluations and organizational audits). I was poisoned and spent a long time in recovery. At that time I wrote non-fiction. That gave me a false impression of how easy it was to become published. I went to the Writers Market, found the companies that seemed to have an interest in what I planned to write, and sent a single paged Tip Sheet outlining my proposal. McFarland, from my original ten, responded and became my non-fiction publisher. I learned that getting published was easy. I recovered from poisoning to the point that I can work again. My "grown up" years gave me insight that I'd missed along the way with respect to people, ripping away the sheltered life I'd lived and exposing me to greed, blind ambition, lie telling, cowardice. It also exposed me to life critical situations: earthquakes and the eruption of Mt. St. Helens where I came close to losing my life in the quicksand along the Toutle River.

All parts of my life have worked together to weave the fabric of The Winds of Change. I began like so many others searching for an agent and/or publisher. The search returned negatives for a wide variety of reasons. It was frustrating. Finally, I remembered hearing about Publication Consultants at an Alaska Writers Guild meeting. I contacted Even Swensen. After all the negatives, I was bowled over when Evan Swensen told me that I had ruined his day. He'd taken my manuscript out of order—something he never does—and began to read and couldn't put it down. I was offered a standard royalty contract and was delighted. My story was rough, to put it nicely. Poisoning had not been kind to my executive function. I had to scramble. A heavy edit took care of the problems and I learned to write better and clean up my mistakes. Ki'ti's Story, 75,000 BC came out in August 2012. I learned in February 2013 that Ki'ti's Story, 75,000 BC, had won a first place award for fiction. Wow! Manak-na's Story, 75,000 BC launched in June 2013.

Finding Publication Consultants is a delightful entré into the world of writing novels for me. They are an easy drive from home. Evan and the staff of Publication Consultants are so very helpful. This is publishing at its best when you can interact with your publisher not only on getting the book out there but also in local efforts: the Alaska Writers Guild, participating in a young writers' conference, and being part of the vast smaller [not an oxymoron] world that is Alaska. It's local even though the distance may be great. I could not have found a better person with whom to share publishing my book. Even Swensen is patient and kind. He is also savvy, making it clear that a writer is also an entrepreneur (wish there was a better word for that).

As I see it, "I've found my niche, and it's a nice one. I'm a workaholic. This is my retirement in Alaska at last, the place I love, where the creation of land is still incredibly obvious. I can write these stories until I die."

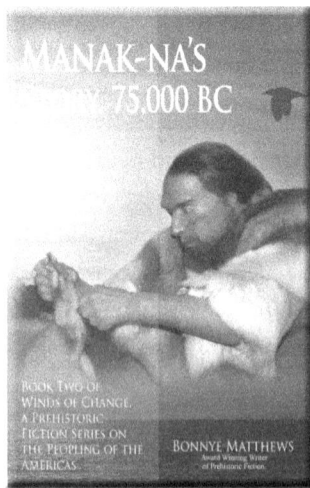

Mama Will You Read To Me
Peggy McMahon

In 2011, when I was ready to publish my two books, I turned to the yellow pages. I had no idea how to go about finding a publisher. Publication Consultants was listed under "Publishers, Book" and I started there. I had self-published my first book *Abba, Hear My Prayers, for Times I Cannot Pray Myself* and it was for sale at Providence Hospital gift shop. I wanted the book to have more of a finished and professional look and be available to a wider audience. The book is a prayer journal I wrote during a serious illness and it is quite personal. Since the book was to be read as a journal I laid it out day by day. I also quoted scripture that supported my journaling. During the editing process I had so many changes: wording, spacing, font, back cover, front cover. You name it, I had it all. Sometimes I didn't know what I wanted until I saw what I didn't want! There were so many changes that I was coming a little bit unglued. But Evan was patient and understanding with me.

My second book, *Father Hear My Psalms, for Times of Prayer and Praise* was somewhat easier, as I knew the process I needed to get a finished book. Writing this book was also very personal as I drew on my spiritual beliefs and based the book on Psalm 23. I would write a psalm and then support it with Bible scripture. I probably proofread it 20 times! Even though my books were very different from the Alaskana books Publication Consultants publishes, I was always made to feel that my books were as valuable as any other book.

My coming-out publication celebration for my second book was at my church and I was so grateful that my church fully supported me. My close friends helped me celebrate and ensured that everything flowed smoothly. There was my banner in the foyer of the church, flowers on my signing table, books spread out, and finger foods for eating. I couldn't have done it on my own; my friends came together to make my initial signing a success. It was an event that brought the community into my church.

There is a special niche for the marketing of these two books. I remember Evan telling me that I would be the one to sell my book, and he was right. Since both books are of a spiritual nature, I turned to Providence Hospital and they agreed to put both books in their gift shop for sale. I have had a slow, but steady request for the books. I wanted a broader audience, so my book was placed on Amazon.com and made available as an eBook. My books still needed exposure. I had to come up with something creative. At the time I did not feel like they were appropriate for a book signing at Costco or Fred Meyer, or other retailers. I had heard that spiritual books are sometimes turned down by certain stores. I may decide in the future that I am ready to pursue signings at these commercial sites.

To reach the religious community I called churches in town and told them about my books. One church bought the books online and invited me to come to their Bible Study where they were using my book. For national exposure, I looked up the websites for all of the Disciples of Christ churches in the country. It turned out to be 40 pages long! I started a slow process of emailing churches, starting with the state of Alabama. I have been surprised again and again at the connections I have with some of the churches across the country. About one in five churches responds and wants to preview the book. I did not write to every church in each state, but selected ones randomly. In the process of doing this I wrote to a church in Southern California and learned that their minister did the memorial service for my father 28 years ago! It's a small world.

I have had ideas about a children's book in my mind for several years. Even though I had ideas, I had no idea how to illustrate it. I contacted Evan for help and he put me in touch with a schoolteacher who is an illustrator. We have had a good time working together; her paintings have captured the story beautifully. I got the inspiration to write my story from my love of books, and how I promoted reading to my children. I read to them every day and I wanted to get the message across to parents that reading to your child is a special and loving thing to do.

The book is appropriate to read to infants, toddlers, and preschoolers. I think that first- and second-graders will be able to read it themselves. It is the story of a mother reading to her little girl. I am now in the process of publishing this children's book, *Mama Will You Read To Me*.

As soon as the paintings were done for the illustrations, they went to the photographer and we will work from there on text placement, color, biography, picture, and other details within the book. With experience from the other two books, I knew more what to expect. I am still quite naïve about marketing and with this third book I will have to reach out to a broader audience than with the first two. I talked with a librarian and gave her the rough draft of the book. She thought it might be appropriate for the "Battle of the Books," a program that wants you to have 2,000 copies ready and available. I would love that! It would give me great exposure in Alaska. I have heard that you sometimes sell more of your first books when you come out with a second or third book.

My book writing is not my "day job." I am a nurse practitioner and I work teaching medical providers, so I sometimes feel very out of the loop in the publishing world. I am learning about marketing and how to become more visible to my target audience. It will be a small victory if I learn how to start a blog and interact with future customers. Right now I have difficulty navigating Facebook so it will be a steep learning curve.

It's exciting to push myself toward new beginnings, so I try not to become discouraged by the marketing aspect of publishing. I believe in what I write and in the end if I make some money from my books, that will be good enough for now.

The Temple
Cameron Mitchell

I have always loved to write. Since I was a kid, I was always sitting at a computer working on something. At one point I even had a really neat typewriter, until I lost it. Or something. Maybe it escaped. I never did find out what happened to that typewriter.

When I was perhaps thirteen years old, I began to think about an idea in my head, which would form the basis for what is now *The Temple*. There were two boys named Halas and Garek, and their father, Harold. Harold was a very stern man, and his sons were far more innocent, naïve to the ways of the world. I knew these characters existed in some sort of fantasy setting. At the time, I was calling the world Cordalis.

I spent the next few years thinking more and more about this idea, the only constant being the names Halas and Garek. I wish I could remember where I came up with these names, but unfortunately I do not.

I was fifteen when I first put my thoughts to the keyboard. The first draft, as to be expected of a fifteen-year-old, was atrocious. I let it sit for a while after maybe thirty pages, and I went back to brainstorming. After a time, I began to fuse the processes. Most of the work still went on in my head, but I began writing and rewriting those first thirty pages. They eventually made their way into what is now *The Temple*. Readers may recall the scene where Halas and his love, Cailin, spend his birthday night outside the forest. That was my first scene.

Much of the writing process was a blur. I would sit down in the latest hours of the night and type away, stopping every so often to pop open another soda.

I wrote most of it during my junior year of high school, while I was being homeschooled, which meant that I could use it to count toward my credits. I finished the book, wrote it again, and decided I was ready for publishing.

I was very wrong.

Over the next year, I would redraft the book again and again, each time deciding that this was the one. I could feel it in my bones. I first sent it off to the publisher Tor/Forge, eager for the acceptance letter I knew was to come.

I was on a big Stephen King kick at the time. He taught me that rejection letters were normal, just par for the course. He wrote about how thrilled he was when his rejection letters started coming back with personal notes, scribbled to him with words of wisdom and encouragement. So imagine my surprise when my very first rejection came in with a few red scribbles at the bottom. I wish I could remember exactly what was written, but it was in the ballpark of, "Maybe not for us right now, but you show a lot of promise. Keep writing, and good luck!"

I had the biggest grin on my face all day.

That was the only time I ever received a personalized rejection. I sent the next few drafts off to different publishers (and two or three more times to Tor/Forge) and all were rejected. I never took it negatively. Each rejection just meant I had to spend another sleepless few weeks writing and polishing. Eventually, my mom approached me. She had a friend who was published with a local group called Publication Consultants. I had never heard of them before. My mother's friend told me that I could do a lot worse. I emailed Evan for the first of many times, asking a bit about the process. He told me to send him my manuscript, and he would see what he could do.

A few days after I had done so he emailed me again. Publication Consultants would publish my book. I was understandably elated.

And then I put it on the back burner. I stopped writing for a while. Some things happened. A few months after my first exchange with Evan, I was hit with that burst of inspiration I absolutely need, and went at *The Temple* once more. I pored over the entire manuscript, adding things I liked, removing things I didn't, and polishing up everything in between. The ending received a complete rewrite. As I was doing that, I realized it was the reason I had lost interest in the book. I had not been happy with my ending. So I scrapped it, and wrote something entirely different. Originally, the Temple of Immortals was much less of a location, and Gilshenn Sidoor's role in the climax was virtually nonexistent.

Finally satisfied with my book, or as satisfied as I was ever going to be ... so I thought at the time. I've since decided that no writer can ever be fully satisfied with his or her book. I emailed Evan again. He said he was still interested in publication, but that our original agreement was for a much smaller manuscript. If I remember correctly, he also mentioned his surprise at how much it had grown since last I showed it to him. But Evan made it work.

A few weeks later I received two boxes filled with copies of *The Temple*, for my release party. It was more surreal than exciting, to see what I had labored so hard for finally come to fruition. I had an actual book in my hands! I could not believe it.

It has been a little over a year since *The Temple* was first published. In that time I have done many signings, and have seen the full spectrum of sales. I have sold nearly fifty copies at Costco, only to turn around and sell only two at Barnes and Noble. They say you have to be prepared to sell as few books as possible, but that is a lesson you can't truly believe until you see it for yourself. It really is a mixed bag. But Evan has organized them all. Words cannot express just how grateful I am for that.

It's like it says on the website: If you have written a book, are writing a book, or are thinking about writing a book, you could certainly do a lot worse than Publication Consultants.

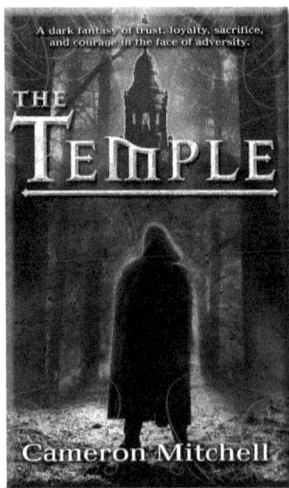

Writing and Publishing a Best Selling Book
Loren Pitchford

If I've heard this statement once, I've heard it a thousand times from various people, at various stages in their lives, who say… … "before I die, I'm going to write a book that gets published." Some even take it a step further and say….. "and my book will become a best seller, and I'll make a pile of money."

In reality only a small fraction of people who make such statements ever publish anything; and out of those individuals, few succeed in actually publishing a book. Why does this happen? In my opinion, it happens because the odds for success are totally stacked against you, whenever you undertake this type of literary endeavor. It takes a substantial amount of time and research; a unique idea; proficiency with personal writing skills; and a little bit of luck to achieve the ultimate goal of publishing a quality book. Even then, the chances remain high that the entire effort may all be in vain, because nobody's interested in what you have to say.

As a writer, if you are willing to take the risk and test the literary market, and then find that the general reading public really is interested in what you have to say, the resultant feeling is the equivalent to winning the literary lottery…especially if your product is a book. Why? Because you will have made an impact in the literary world and your book will become a legacy in time about who you are and what you stand for. That's what happened with my first non-fiction Alaska fishing book, *Real Alaskan Fish Tales*. It was a major personal undertaking that took years to complete, but ultimately had a great pay off. As a consequence, I'd like to offer a few "words of wisdom" about how I finally arrived at the "finish line" of my long literary journey, and a few of the problems and obstacles that occurred along the way. If you are an aspiring writer, I am hopeful that this advice will be of benefit, because I learned most of my lessons from actual experiences over a considerable period of time.

I believe that everybody should have a few passions in life. Passions are things you enjoy doing and they never seem to diminish over time. They are usually things that peak your interest and encourage you to become more proficient in the particular craft. As years pass, such passions seem to grow and so does your proficiency. I have a number of passions I have pursued most of my life. One is fishing and another is writing. I've spent 50 years perfecting my fishing skills and 30 years writing about my fishing experiences. I never get tired of doing either of these passions because I've always enjoyed them.

If you believe you have a passion for writing, then you need to answer a few basic questions about your chosen craft. Do I enjoy doing it? Will I spend the necessary time and effort doing it? And, will I probably want to do it forever? If the answer to any of the above is "No" then writing for you is really not a passion, it is more like a job. Nobody likes a job because jobs have restrictions, rules and timetables. Passions don't.

If you passed the first test on being a writer, here's the second test. Do I have the necessary skills and mindset to do the job? Many established authors have big egos because they believe in themselves and their writing abilities. They also believe that what they have to say will readily be accepted by others. The only way to find out if this premise is true is to write something and see if a publisher will accept it

I recommend starting small (i.e. articles) before you attempt to go large (i.e. a book). It takes less time and effort, and hopefully gives you an expedited answer to the question. Publishers of both magazines and books are in the literary business to make money. They want to market articles and books that will sell. If you have name recognition and credentials from past publications, you are usually *in*. If not, you will definitely be *out* and probably receive rejection notices or nothing at all.

Remember, if you believe in yourself you can win, but you will never win unless you are willing to try. I was fortunate in my literary endeavors. Over a twenty year timeframe, I submitted more than 40 feature articles, with accompanying photos and illustrations, to various outdoor magazine publishers in Alaska and the Lower 48. All of my submissions were accepted and published. I never got rich from any of these publications even though a few of my photos appeared on magazine covers and many articles were features; but I did establish a reading audience as well as writer's credentials. I believe such credentials and reading audience are necessary if you are going to write and publish a book. The time and effort required for a book is substantial and so are the corresponding financial requirements to develop a quality product. No publishing house in today's financial environment is going to risk their capital on you or your book unless they firmly believe that your work will create a potential profit for them. You must also understand that you are competing against an army of other authors and writers who want to accomplish the same goal you do. As a consequence, I believe it is important to create your own writer's niche which will make your work different from all the rest. My niche was Alaska fishing stories that contained adventure, close calls, how to information and humor. I also created my own captioned illustrations to supplement the text.

Many authors hit a stone wall with established book publishers after making numerous manuscript submissions and receiving continual rejections. As a result they end up with a vanity press approach which means self publishing. This can be difficult terrain in any writer's literary journey because you are now putting your own money behind your words and ideas. You have to ask the question …. "Do I have enough capital to cover the costs of editing, proofing, printing, distribution, marketing and promotion?" Contractor help is available, but there's always a price tag for all of their services.

When it comes time to present your finished product to the public, I may be old-fashioned but I believe that a book should have a hard cover and be something that an individual holds in their hands and turns pages while it's being read. In this day of modern technology, many people would disagree with that belief and feel that the only way to purchase a book is through the Internet, using special applications to access the text. From a marketing standpoint, you can reach a much larger reading audience through the Internet since most people rely on computers for communications and entertainment. As an author, you need to decide what works best for you.

Once you have published a book, whether it's in hard copy or disc form, the last literary hurdle that remains is public acceptance of your finished product. This is where the rubber really hits the road. If you correctly calculated all the risks, then the rewards should be forthcoming in book sales, after your finished product hits the market. If that happens, you've won the literary lottery! You will be recognized as an established author and soon find that the rewards and opportunities just keep coming. For someone with a passion for writing, it doesn't get any better than that.

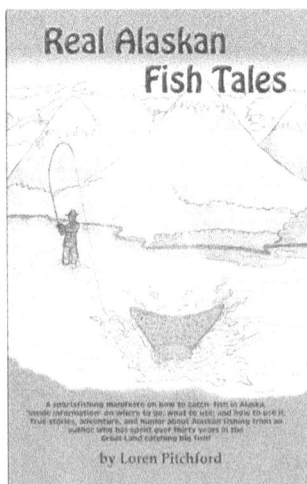

On Coincidences
Mary Ann Poll

There is one thing to be said for coincidences. There aren't any. And before you think I'm crazy or just narrow-minded, consider the following story of how I became a published author.

A day came when I was confronted with an indisputable fact: My eternal soul lives in nothing more than crockery. That day came in May 1998.

I awoke for another day of work. Hands reaching toward the ceiling in that wonderful morning stretch were stopped instantly by sharp, tear-producing pain. As the initial pain subsided, I downed a pain reliever and was at my desk by 9 a.m. The pain returned with a vengeance by noon. At 1 p.m. I found myself in the emergency room. A disc had herniated in my neck and I faced surgery with a long recovery.

This small writing sample is from a piece I wrote several years ago when I was asked to describe how I became an author. As they say, "The Lord works in mysterious ways." Indeed, He does. Because if a disc in my neck had not herniated, if I had not read 100 books in ninety days because I could do nothing else while I healed, and if I had not listened to a good friend who suggested I write a novel, I would not be writing this story today.

My first book in what is now the *Iconoclast* series took many more years before it saw the black and white of printing. That journey was full of trips down other paths—going back to work time and again to make the almighty dollar and avoid the emotions and mental weariness that writing took. I took courses, joined online chat groups and talked about writing until I was blue in the face. In the end, I accepted that the idea of writing was not going to go away. That was the day I sat down to write a book. It took twelve years to summon the courage and face the passion that would not leave, no matter what I did.

In all the trips down other pathways, one helped me. I found out about National Novel Writing Month from a contact I made on a Christian writers forum. This is a yearly event where more than 300,000 writers come together and grind out a novel in 30 days. I had tried everything else, so what was there to lose? So I committed to the project. Lo and behold, *Ravens Cove* was born.

Once it was written, I was faced with the frightening and somewhat overwhelming question every writer has: "What now?" My answer for several months was, "Nothing!" This was when I first discovered that writing a book is akin to giving birth. I wasn't putting my "baby" out into the world for criticism and rejection.

So, I let the book sit in the dark for several months. It stayed in the rawest of formats and I think I was actually in denial that I had written an entire novel. I didn't have (or make) the time to edit it because I had no clue where to go and who to trust with my baby.

My husband read the prologue and told me it was great. Of course he did. He wanted dinner and to sleep in his own bed—what else could he say? I knew he meant it. I also knew he loved me so I dismissed his compliment.

My father-in-law came to visit the summer after I wrote *Ravens Cove*. He asked if I might allow him to read it. His reading it was not such a frightening thought and, to be honest, I really wanted his opinion. And I trusted his view because he has a PhD in education and had published works of his own. He also happened to be the most avid reader I had ever met.

I gave him the book. He and my husband left that weekend for our RV in Anchor Point. He read it there. He came back and told me he really liked it. He said he had read authors he thought should have never been published. And he thought my book should be.

My husband, with the I-told-you-so-look, agreed. Then he took it a step further and emailed links to several publishers and publishing houses with information on what it took to get the book to press. Here's where providence is again disguised as coincidence. One of those names was Publication Consultants.

I debated sending out query letters to the "big houses." I heard stories of books that were tied up for months, even a year or more, by those big publishing houses that had initially accepted the author's work and then left them hanging forever. I debated the self-publishing houses and again read and heard of the horror stories of authors that were taken financially to the point it wasn't worthwhile to pursue marketing their books. With all this I decided I wanted to be able to look a publisher in the eye. So I met with Evan Swensen of Publication Consultants.

Evan reviewed the first few pages of what was to be *Ravens Cove*. There were some problems but he told me the story was good and he would publish it—after I took it to an editor to fix the "boulders"—his word for problems. The rest is history. Since 2010, I have been privileged to call Publication Consultants my publishing house.

Publication Consultants was and still is invaluable to this author. They have taught, and are still teaching me the ins and outs of the road to becoming a successful author. There have been numerous mountains to climb and valleys to traverse. They have stuck with me throughout the process and have opened doors that self-publishing could not. Without Evan Swensen and his staff, I would not have reached the goal of becoming a published author.

As I stated when I began this story, there are no coincidences. Each occurrence that seemed so small in and of itself led me to Publication Consultants and the adventure of being a published author. To date, the journey continues with a third book in the *Iconoclast* series in draft. And when ready and God willing, it will come to maturity with the assistance of Publication Consultants.

Little Old Ladies Came in Off the Street
Dolores Roguszka

My publication career did not begin with Evan Swensen but had its start some 50 years before we ever met. At that time I was a professional photographer and budding writer, selling articles to magazines such as *The Alaska Sportsman* for the remarkable fees of ½ cent a word plus $5 for one-time use of an 8-by-10 black and white glossy photograph! I had my share of rejection slips but I also sold my packages of text and photos on a regular basis. Frankly, I'm sure it was my photography that tipped the scales toward sales and I urge every writer to provide good photo coverage to accompany their prose. Either learn to do your own photography (easier today with digital cameras than it was in yesteryears) or find other sources for illustrations.

During the 1960s I was a regular contributor to the *Alaska Sportsman*, continuing even with their fee schedule. At the time of the 1964 earthquake the *Sportsman* publisher requested an article and photos covering the big event. He would "hold the presses" until it arrived! I dropped everything else in order to produce this feature story. Alas, that was before the days of electronic technology permitting instant transfers of text and photos . . . and my article did not arrive soon enough. Other material was used in their earthquake edition. The presses were not stopped long enough! And so the document sat in my files until I met Jan Boylan, some 40 years later.

My career as author and photographer continued and ultimately my work appeared in more than 50 different publications in the United States and Europe. I never contemplated writing a book.

In the early 1980s I taught photography at UCLA, first being asked to fill in for another instructor, whose schedule unexpectedly changed. That class was successful and I then agreed to continue teaching for the next several years. During that time I was requested by Amphoto Publications to write one of their planned "Amphoto Guide" series books. Believe me, a rare occurrence! In the usual chain of events a writer asks for publication of his book, but is not given a contract to produce one. I chose to write a book for beginning photographers that I could use as a text for my classes. This was an easy one to write because the subject was one I knew well. A tough editor who was the published author of several photography books himself insisted on changes. Like most writers, I resisted having to change my perfect prose. Only after the book was published did I agree that he was right and I was wrong! Even now, after all these years, I still resent it when an editor makes changes. I've had enough experience now not to be so stubborn though, and submit a little easier. The outcome was a book entitled *Amphoto Guide to SLR Photography*, featuring my photos as well as those of my students, including several 4-H members I had mentored in our local 4-H group. I was pleased with the book, although it never hit the best-seller list! It did work well as a text.

Back in Alaska in 2003 I read an item by Janet Boylan in the Anchorage Senior Center newsletter requesting personal earthquake stories from members to be made into some kind of publication. Jan was motivated to raise money for the center and was convinced that a collection of personal earthquake experiences might fill the bill. I had never met Jan but called her to ask if my long-ago-filed copy might be helpful.

We met and talked. Jan's original idea had been of a ring-bound, house-produced book or booklet. We talked some more. I agreed to work with her to produce a book, but only if we could produce one of substance and worthy of such a historical event. She was happy to head in that direction. We started to collect stories. My unpublished article written for the *Alaska Sportsman* became the lead story in our book. If it *had* been published 40 years before, this book, in its present form, would never have been written. Fate does act kindly. Once in a while.

During the year we worked. Collecting, refining, and becoming more and more excited with the results, until we finally decided we had enough for a book and it was time to find a publisher. Where in Anchorage, Alaska, do you find a publisher? You start with the Yellow Pages, of course. Neither of us knew anything about any of those listed so we started at the top of the list and made appointments to consult.

The first few local interviews were pretty dismal. No interest. *Very* expensive quotes. No encouragement. "Leave your name and number and we'll get back to you!" Of course, we never heard from these outfits. We *knew* we had something good but did no one else recognize the potential? Some very discouraging appointments. Working our way down the list we reached Publication Consultants, located on some strange-sounding street we'd never heard of. A city map helped to find it and we headed for our appointment, manuscript and photos in hand, to see Evan Swensen.

And what a difference in our reception! Evan and Lois actually acted as if they were happy to see us. Since Evan had lived through the 1964 earthquake in Anchorage and had his own story to tell (he was manager of the local Montgomery Ward store at the time) he could see the merit in our collection of stories. This experience was everything the others were not!

We explained that the purpose of this book was two-fold: one, to preserve some Alaska history heretofore not written and two, to make money for the Senior Center. Neither Jan nor I have ever charged one dime for our efforts on this project.

At that first meeting Evan described to us his methods possible for publishing a book; gave us suggestions as to what we needed to add to our manuscript; helped us make decisions as to how many books to order for this first printing and generally supported, enthusiastically, our mission. I must say, of *all* the publishers I've known, Evan is by far the easiest I've ever worked with. And *always* with good humor! This man must have a bad day now and then, but I've never seen it.

Receiving this first shipment of books was absolutely thrilling. We had accomplished our first goal, and were overjoyed with it. Now we needed to move forward with the second. Evan not only helped us before printing, but continues to assist sales in the form of setting up book signings and writer's conferences for us and for his other authors. Pep talks and useful information are a part of the tasty taco dinners he and Lois host in their home for all of us.

Our book signings have been successful. I'll never forget Evan's comments during the first signing following publication " ...These two little old ladies came in off the street, not knowing what they were doing ... and they produced a best seller!" Our book has sold well. We're now into the sixth printing. Sales have slowed a bit but as long as we can be out there signing books, we'll continue to sell. Books don't necessarily sell books—people sell books!

Evan and Lois continue to assist writers to become published authors. Gracious, honest, helpful, encouraging, competent, and always with a smile and great good humor. I treasure them as friends.

No, my first publication was not with Evan Swensen, but now at 82 years of age I can proudly say that *The Day Trees Bent to the Ground* is the one I'm most proud of. The Senior Center has, to date, benefited by more than $40,000 in royalties alone.

My advice, if you've written a book, if you're writing a book, or if you're thinking about writing a book, go *first* to Publication Consultants. You'll be glad you did!

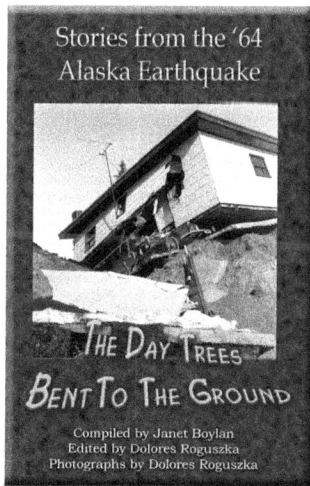

Stories from the '64 Alaska Earthquake

THE DAY TREES BENT TO THE GROUND

Compiled by Janet Boylan
Edited by Dolores Roguszka
Photographs by Dolores Roguszka

As I Breathe, I Write
Marianne Schlegelmilch

I have long found it amusing when people ask me how long I have been writing. My standard tongue-in-cheek answer is this: *As I breathe, I write.*

I write often, I write prolifically, and I write even when a phone call would be faster. Just ask my publisher, who often comments on how many emails I send. I simply just love to write—but personal and selective writing, for I don't do social media, and that's a whole other story.

Writing has always been easy for me. Perhaps it is because my mother was a newspaperwoman—working as a reporter at our hometown newspaper in her days before marrying my father, and later rising to the esteemed level of head obituary writer, a position that earned her the title, *Obit Lucy.* She always stressed grammar and spelling. Interesting that after such intense, personal training, I have trouble with both of those today.

In nursing school, I wrote humorous songs and ditties to help get me through the serious business of my studies. And later, as a practicing critical care nurse, I wrote poetry and essays to relieve the immense stress of dealing with life and death issues every day.

It was during my work as a nurse that I first became a published author and first met Evan Swensen of Publication Consultants. Someone had jokingly suggested a children's book for a fundraiser at the Blood Bank of Alaska, where I worked. The subject had come up during one of those impromptu brainstorming sessions that workplaces in America are known for, and so, when the subject came up, I jumped on it, saying without hesitation, "I can do this!"

And I did do it, creating the fictional story of a small puppy found by race founder Joe Redington Sr., who learns all about the Iditarod and even more about life. A coworker did the wonderful and thoughtful illustrations and cover, and I had no trouble getting my story done once my life coach, mentor, and lifelong loving husband, Bill, told me I could do it, and even came up with more than a few great ideas.

What I wasn't prepared for was editing. Another coworker edited my work. She had the credentials for sure, but I was fully convinced that she was homogenizing my work and removing all traces of "me" from my writing. I found it very difficult to absorb. And then there was the boss's wife, who didn't think the spelling of the title was tasteful. Well, I won that small battle when I pointed out that I had named the book after my own dog, whose registered name was just as I spelled it on the title.

And, I have to admit that the editor did a fine job, now that I have reread the book some ten years later. In retrospect, I so appreciate the dedication of everyone involved in providing all their input to help create a successful project. They could have thrown me out there flailing, but they helped polish me and let me shine. Thus, my first book, *Solo Flite*, was published in 2002.

By all accounts it was a success, even raising enough to donate a portion of the profits to Joe Redington's widow, Vi, to help her dream of building a museum to the sport of mushing in which to house her late husband's memories. Words cannot say how important it was to me to keep this small promise to her to thank her and Joe and their family for their support of my fledgling writing endeavor and my work in managing the first satellite center of the Blood Bank of Alaska—something they were instrumental in helping to promote.

After that experience, I figured I was done. I had a book out and it had done well, but I was a nurse and I had to work, so no more serious thoughts of writing emerged. That is, until around 2006, when some serious life challenges prompted me to again want to diffuse my stress and try to move others to care.

This time I wrote for veterans—veterans with PTSD, one of whom I was married to. I wanted people to understand that these soldiers of war were good people whose lives would never be the same because of their service to our country. They had made the hidden sacrifice of self—serving honorably and with valor, and now left carrying a lifetime of pain.

Inspired by the ravens that frequent the Mat-Su Valley in the winter, I wrote *Raven's Light*—the fictional tale of a raven named Zak, who faces his own traumas and resolutions after witnessing masses of his friends die in Alaska's biggest oil spill.

I was as surprised as anyone that the story came out in two voices and became an allegorical story of PTSD, written as a tale of nine months in an Alaska winter, and featuring characters who I named after veterans with PTSD that I knew.

Most people didn't see the deeper story, seeing only a colorful local tale, but for those who did, it was powerful. I know this because they told me. The vets said I got it right, and other readers said it changed their lives. One woman vowed to carry it to the top of Mount McKinley during a future climb she was planning in memory of her son who was lost at war. Later, I would be devastated after what I thought was a successful book signing at an iconic bookstore in Anchorage led to one of their staff's trashing my most personal and difficult-to-write book on a public website. To this day, I ask why?

My spirits were lifted, though, as I met more of those who said the book touched them like no other book had ever done. A few nationally prominent figures embraced it, telling me they wanted to share my book with others. I decided that the bookseller who chose to trash it just didn't get it. Still, I really never got over the insensitivity or the wondering why someone would go out of his way to hurt someone. Nurses, you see, have trouble with meanness.

I wrote another tale in two voices and dedicated it to a friend whose wife had died young. I started a third tale, but it is incomplete. Somewhere along the way, I observed that mysteries seemed to do well, so I wrote one, then two, and now three. Even within the story lines of my mysteries, people keep telling me I touch them. It is a great compliment—better than money.

I like to think I can write anything I want to. I believe that. Perhaps it is arrogance. I don't consider it confidence, for I am fully convinced that I am not really successful. I do know that my writing touches people. Is that success? Maybe it is and maybe it is just the feeding of my insatiable need to express myself.

I am working on my fourth mystery and a couple of other projects. I write a column for the Alaska Nurses Association called, *Heart of the Alaska Nurse*. Nurses tell me they love it—high-up nurses who never before knew my name. Who knew?

They, too, say my writing touches them. They call me a leader. There is a book in the works. I am donating my work to an already established fund set up to help nurses. Again I ask, "Who knew?" I have a coauthor. I hope to help her shine in her first book as well.

I suppose I will always write, just as I will always wonder if I am tying up unnecessary resources to have my books published. I dread book signings, but yet I always seem to enjoy them once I'm there. People talk to me, I listen, and we share.

The hard issues of money and sales distress me. I don't like to deal with money issues. I never have. I try hard, though, in spite of it, and I try to help other authors succeed. For me, it's not about the money, although I do love those royalty checks.

I love to brainstorm, too—to find creative ways to succeed. Perhaps I like to challenge myself to succeed. I think it keeps me on my toes, especially the rejections—the not wanting to carry my books, or the rare bad review. They make me mad and disappointed and hurt, but ultimately they make me try harder and appreciate the good things that come my way.

As has often been said, *For every door that closes, a new one opens.* I like to think that way, although waiting to find that right door is as maddening and demoralizing as I can imagine. Thus, to use another cliché, I *keep on keeping on.* I hope I always will. I am grateful to have a supportive husband and to have a publisher who tries to inspire. I am an author. Again I say, "Who knew?"

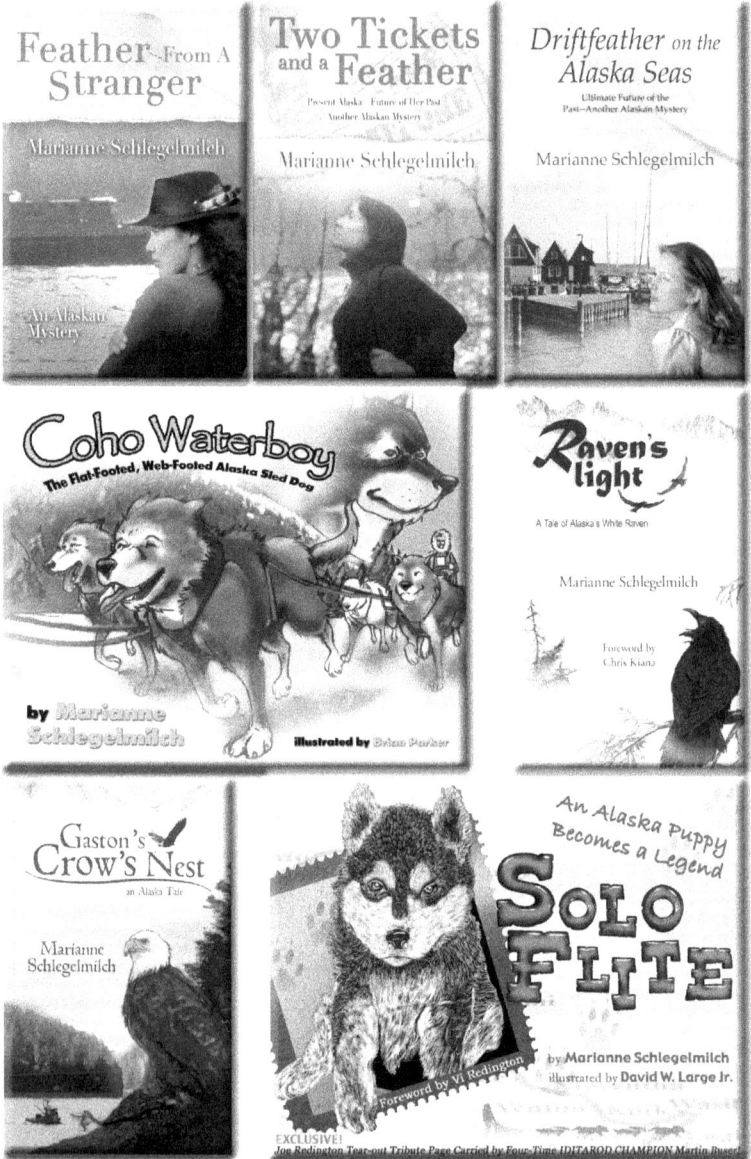

Feather From A Stranger

Marianne Schlegelmilch

An Alaskan Mystery

Two Tickets and a Feather

Present Alaska - Future of Her Past
Another Alaskan Mystery 2

Marianne Schlegelmilch

Driftfeather on the Alaska Seas

Ultimate Future of the
Past—Another Alaskan Mystery

Marianne Schlegelmilch

Coho Waterboy

The Flat-Footed, Web-Footed Alaska Sled Dog

by Marianne Schlegelmilch

illustrated by Brian Parker

Raven's light

A Tale of Alaska's White Raven

Marianne Schlegelmilch

Foreword by
Chris Kiana

Gaston's Crow's Nest

an Alaska Tale

Marianne
Schlegelmilch

Solo Flite

An Alaska Puppy
Becomes a Legend

by Marianne Schlegelmilch
illustrated by David W. Large Jr.

Foreword by Vi Redington

EXCLUSIVE!
Joe Redington Tear-out Tribute Page Carried by Four-Time IDITAROD CHAMPION Martin Buser

Sweet Slice of Fear
Jim Seckler

I started writing stories right around the time I graduated from high school. Before that I wrote Bob Dylan-like song lyrics, more like prose. It was a few years later when the horror movie *The Exorcist* came out, which influenced me to write a novel. My first attempt was a novella about an evil basilisk that terrorized Salt Lake City. The book was bad and dejectedly I started writing short stories. My favorite author is Ernest Hemingway so I read everything he wrote. I wrote a dozen or so short stories, each one just a little better that the last.

One of Hemingway's books, *A Farewell to Arms*, influenced me to write my next novel, a historical story about an American cowboy who travels to the Ottoman Empire in 1874. I followed that book up with two sequels; the last of the trilogy was my longest novel at 110,000 words about the Armenian massacres of 1915.

Told that I should write about what I know, I wrote another contemporary novel about working at a manufacturing company in Southern California. I then moved up to the Seattle area and got the idea to write a story about a bachelor who finds himself adopting three children. The idea came after I had bought three acres of wooded rural land west of Seattle. It was about that time I completely rewrote the first novella about the evil basilisk and changed it to a novel about two female serial killers.

While living in Oregon, I went back to college and received a journalism degree at the University of Oregon. That education taught me how to write much better than I had been writing. Plus, once I started working as a reporter, I could now say that I wrote for a living. After two newspaper jobs in Northern California, I landed in Northern Arizona where I now work as a crime and county government reporter for a newspaper in Bullhead City. It was at a local bookstore that I met Don Porter, who was signing books. Picking his brain about how to get published, he told me about Publication Consultants, a publisher in Alaska. I sent them the manuscript about the female serial killers, which they turned down. I then sent them the manuscript about the bachelor who adopted the three children. That became *Sweet Slice of Fear*. I have since written a sequel to *Sweet Slice of Fear* and have finished another thriller about an antigovernment ex-soldier who goes on a killing spree.

Since my first attempt at writing, I have sent query letters to publishers and agents getting little feedback and plenty of rejections. I am still getting rejected for everything I have written, except for *Sweet Slice of Fear*.

I found that writing is a two-pronged endeavor. The first is getting published and the second is marketing the book once you do. Many writers self-publish their books but they still end up marketing their books themselves.

With millions of writers out there soliciting a handful of publishers and agents to take on their works, the competition is stiff to get published by a large enough publisher. The same can be said about agents. I have tried to get an agent in the past and fell victim to two agents who asked me for money for some kind of fee and did little or no work to find a publisher. I lost several hundred dollars to those agents.

Living in a small town and working full-time makes it very hard to market *Sweet Slice of Fear*. I tried to market it through newspaper articles, radio interviews, several book signings and by using Facebook and Linked-in and the Internet. A friend even made a video on YouTube about it. Being lucky is a prerequisite to getting published. Living temptingly close to Las Vegas or Laughlin, I realize that I am not very lucky. The *Twilight* series written by a Phoenix woman was rescued off the slush pile.

I also tried my hand at writing a screenplay about a black journalist who worked at a Los Angeles newspaper from 1910 to 1950. I read about her true story in one of my journalism books. Trying to sell a screenplay is also impossible. My cousin's daughter once worked for and still knows

Jennifer Garner and Ben Affleck but even that was not enough to get anyone's attention to the screenplay. I have written to Oprah Winfrey, Spike Lee, Morgan Freeman, and Melissa Perry-Harris about this black journalist's incredible and interesting story of fighting against racism and for civil rights in LA in the early part of the 20th century.

To date, I have sold about 120 books of *Sweet Slice of Fear*. Even though people say I have published a novel, I still feel unfulfilled knowing that I have spent endless hours after my regular job working on my writing for not only years but decades. I have written a total of eight novels, a novella, a screenplay and a dozen short stories but published only one book.

The only thing I ever wanted to do is write and make a comfortable living doing that full-time. I also want to be considered a good writer. I recommend writers to have someone read and edit their work before submitting it. *Sweet Slice of Fear* was not edited by anyone except for myself and there are many mistakes in it still after I edited it literally dozens of times. Its sequel was edited by four people and I think it's a much better book.

Writers should also take writing classes at a college as well as read published authors, something I am guilty of not doing very much. Going to writers conferences is also a good idea. In the end, having a manuscript rescued off a slush pile is a spin of the roulette wheel.

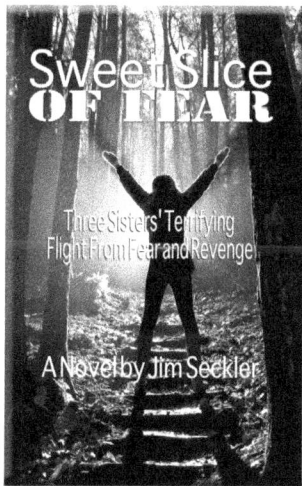

Talking With God
Dena Sessler

Oh, to be an Author! To touch and impact lives through my words was a dream ever since I was a little girl, but life seems to have a way of going in a direction that you don't anticipate!

My journey to become an author has been a long, painful road but a spiritual one. I have had a life full of disappointment, devastation, and abuse. People talk about being dealt a bad hand of cards—well, I felt that I was given a bad deck. Nothing seemed to be going right and I found myself on the "pity pot" for way too long questioning and asking "Why me!"

I grew up in the beautiful state of Alaska, where I still reside. My father was a very religious and hardworking man who was rarely available; my mother had a difficult time showing me any love because of her childhood, and was addicted to whatever drug was fashionable at the time to help her cope with life; and a younger sister grew up thinking she was a princess and should have the world given to her. I had to grow up quick taking care of my family in the ways that my mother was incapable of. That is when I started to write poetry as a way to pass the many hours I spent alone and express my feelings, if only on paper, for my eyes only to see.

I went to college and took many courses on creative writing and poetry, and read books on becoming an author and publishing your book. It left me overwhelmed and confused. To make matters worse, I had a college professor tell me that I would never be a published author, at least with poetry, and I needed to consider writing for Hallmark because my poetry was too rhythmic and flowery. Wow, did that cut deep! Instead of viewing her opinion as just that, an opinion, I let her comment define who I was for the next 27 years, embarrassed about sharing my writing with anyone.

I went through life rolling with the punches and saying to myself "God doesn't give us more than we can handle," and "What doesn't kill us makes us stronger!" There is a lot of truth in those statements; however, if you allow it to, it will beat you down and take away any amount of worth that you have.

I have had many careers throughout my life, including everything from high-fashion runway modeling in California to heavy equipment operating on the North Slope of Alaska. In 1999 I thought I was doing a pretty good job at managing my life, considering what I had endured up to this point, and felt blessed to be alive. I was living large and had the world in my hands, making a six-figure income a year. God had different plans for me though! In July 1999 I suffered a severe cerebral stroke that was sure to end my life. It went misdiagnosed for more than seven hours. The doctors were sure that I had overdosed on drugs, even though the toxicology report was negative for even aspirin. After all, I was a healthy 31-year-old woman who was too young to suffer a stroke, so I had to be doing street drugs that they couldn't detect.

I was sent to the hospital on Elmendorf for supportive care. When I got there, it was apparent to them that it wasn't a drug overdose at all and I was suffering a severe stroke. When the MRI came back, it was confirmed, but by that time my brain damage was so severe that they were sure I would suffer a brain stem hemorrhage and not survive the night. My family was called in to say their final goodbyes and a military chaplain to administer last rites.

When I awoke the next morning, to their surprise, my family was told I would never walk or talk again. I had lost 40 per cent of my cerebellum and the prognosis was not good. God proved them wrong again. The doctors had no medical explanation as to why I didn't die that night. They were amazed at the fact that I was able to understand them or even attempt to stand with help. They racked it up to a medical miracle but my belief was different. You see, God has a plan for everyone, even though it may not be obvious at the time.

I remember when it first happened; I started to pray to God that nothing was seriously wrong with me. Then lying in the hospital, experiencing the worst pain and suffering imaginable, I prayed for him to take my life because it was more than I could bear. In most military hospitals, or so my family was told, pain killers were not administered to a patient who had no hope of survival. The pain of my brain swelling was excruciating and the only comfort I received was nurses wiping my frail body down with cool rags. I couldn't help but think if there was a God, why had he forsaken me? Why was he letting me suffer the way I was? Why wouldn't he listen to my prayers? Because of my upbringing, I was convinced that I had done something terribly wrong to upset God and I was being punished.

I spent the next two years learning how to walk again, tie my shoes, feed myself, talk, drive, and the list goes on and on. How humbling for someone who had a class A CDL with every endorsement available! The cerebellum is considered the "little brain" and stores learned skills. Even though I knew how to do the simplest of things, my body would not comply. I had to go through every step in my mind and force my body to respond, until it became second nature again. It was a long and frustrating process. I had a lot of time to build up a plethora of feelings. Happiness to be alive, pity for myself because I would never be able to hold a job again, and anger with God.

During those two years, not everything was bad. Life did start to turn around. I met my incredible husband in December 1999, shortly after my stroke. I came to find out years later that he had called his mother and told her that he met the most beautiful woman. When asked what my name was, he replied "I don't know, I can't understand a single thing she says! It was her smile and the incredible sparkle she had in her eyes that got my attention!" It wouldn't be too long before I lost both again. In the next few years I underwent seven major surgeries, open heart being the worst, and two high-risk pregnancies.

In 2003 and 2005 we were blessed with two beautiful boys. Life was getting good again. Here God gave me two boys when the doctors said I wouldn't be able to have children. Then a new set of challenges began. Our oldest son was diagnosed with autism and our youngest had severe ADHD and was bipolar. I thought "Okay, you have to be kidding me! God must see a strength I don't because I don't think I can take anymore!"

I started to write again, with new motivation, a way to touch and reach my boys. I now had this belief that I had to start doing everything possible to make God happy so he would stop punishing me. I drove my health and family into the ground with my volunteering and quest for acceptance with the Lord. Boy, did I have it wrong! It wasn't until four years ago that a friend from church said to me "Your pain has become your identity. The Lord doesn't work that way and you are his incredible masterpiece. Turn everything over to him and ask for guidance. He has an incredible plan for you, so stop searching and ask the one who knows! There is a reason you have gone through what you have so find a way to see the blessings in it." I thought, "Yeah right! I've been there done that and it doesn't work. Find the blessings, you have to be kidding me!"

I spent the next few years doing a lot of work on myself. I started to share my poetry with my husband and trusted friends. I would write touching poetry for birthdays, weddings, classes, and funerals with beautiful response. I thought to myself, maybe there is something to this.

My mother had been battling cancer for 14 years, but in June 2011 started to rapidly lose her fight. I found myself being a caregiver, trying to take care of a family and two boys with special needs, and continue what I thought was the Lord's work and the direction he wanted me to go. In September 2011 I wrote another poem for my son who was struggling with the fact that he had autism and why God had made him that way. What I didn't know was that this was the beginning of the incredible children's book that was soon to follow. I remember praying to God that night. I said "Lord, I know this can't be what you want for me, a life of suffering and service with no joy. I am your servant, please use me as your tool for your glory! Show me what it is you would have me do and I will do my best to obey!"

I came home late one night in October, exhausted from the events of the day and caring for my mother. My family was in bed so I made a cup of tea, went outside, and tried to relax for just a minute. I had an indescribable desire to start to write, so I went in and grabbed a pen and paper and started. It was as though the Lord himself was telling me what to write and I just moved the pen. Three and one-half hours later I went to bed, excited to share with my husband the next evening what had happened and the beautiful poetry that seemed to just pour out of me that night. The next day, to my disappointment, I couldn't find my notebook. My husband told me to just write it again. I told him, "You don't understand! I can't remember what I wrote!" It was extremely uncharacteristic for me, not to be able to recite verbatim something I had written or said. I spent three days tearing the house apart looking for it. I found it in my youngest son's room, covered with pictures of God, robots, cars, and flowers. Instead of getting angry I thought, I get it, you want this book to be illustrated by children. So I went to Eagle River Christian School where my boys attend and asked the children for artwork.

What followed was a wave of excitement. I went looking for a publisher! Everything I had read up to this point about publishing your book led me to believe that it would be easy. I couldn't have been more wrong. It is easy enough to find a list of publishers online; however, in my experience they either want your money, all the control, or your book outright. This left me upset and frustrated. I wanted to find someone who believed in me, my vision, and was honest and virtuous. I found that in Evan at Publication Consultants. Not only was I supporting a local business, but Evan got it! He could see my vision, was compassionate, encouraging, and helpful. He never tried to take control of me and my book, only giving gentle suggestions and sound advice. Evan led me, every step of the way, through the process of getting my book published. Wow, a publisher who actually cared about me, the author, and my book was something that I hadn't been expecting. Evan has been there to hold my hand, explain things to me, share in my frustration and excitement, and was always available to his authors.

This part of my story and journey is now coming to an end, but I know the best is yet to come. More books are in my future, and Evan and Publication Consultants will be right there with me! It is difficult to capture one's life in 2,500 words, but I have shared parts of my life to give you inspiration, encouragement, and hope. It's not meant to minimize your own story, but to share with you my struggles and challenges, realizing now that God can take even the most broken life and turn it into something beautiful. You see, God doesn't answer prayers the way we think they should be answered or submit to the pressures of our impatience. It is said that "the truth will set you free." Well, so will getting rid of all the garbage and baggage that we carry with us through our lives. For me, my writers block wasn't lifted until I dealt with and rid myself of the anger, resentment, hurt, and pain that I had been carrying with me for way too long. Healing my relationship with the Lord, my image of myself and relationships with others was also imperative to smooth out the bumps and craters in my path. It has taken more than 40 years, but I finally got the answers to the burning questions I had for so many years. A published author of spiritual poetry for children. Wow, didn't see that one coming!

My advice to anyone wanting to become an author is this: don't let anyone define you. Hold tight to your dreams. Get your thoughts down on paper. Don't allow anyone to compromise or change your vision, and find a publisher who cares about you!

Many blessing to you all and the best of wishes to you on your journey to becoming an author and the success and joy that is undoubtedly coming your way!

I Love Writing
Esther Smith

I love writing! Since I was old enough to put a crayon to paper, I have always enjoyed creating stories, divulging feelings, and recording facts on paper through word or art. I think at least since age 10, I was determined to be an author—however, at that age I never could have imagined that my first published piece of work would be a book about potty training for children.

Seventeen years later, I had three children, all with autism, and all in diapers. Toilet training was very important to me and was on my mind more than frequently. It was almost constantly! I had bought, borrowed, or rented about every book or toy available at the time that pertained at all to potty training. Nothing worked.

I wanted to relax and do something that I enjoyed. I needed to take a much-needed break from such stress that most cannot imagine. There was no way to justify such a luxury when I was finishing my bachelor's degree in visual communications, my husband was completing his degree in business management and information systems, he was working full time, and we had three children—who were smearing poop on the walls, beating their heads into things, eating sheetrock and wood right off the walls and the windowsills, and so on.

Finally, at a complete loss and in meltdown myself one day after my 3-year-old daughter had stripped naked at a grocery store and screamed so loud that an old lady had accused me of kidnapping and I had to leave without even buying my groceries, I dropped by my bedside and fell on my knees. I am a religious person, and have been my whole life. I knew how to pray and had prayed oh so often, but I had never before "cried unto the Lord" the way I did that afternoon.

This time I got an answer. The answer was just a thought in a weary mind that could not have thought of anything but sleep, help, and rest from my troubles at that moment. Yet, this thought was clear and confident, not my own thought. It plainly came as a question. "Why not use your talents, hobbies, and skills to both give yourself a break and improve your situation?"

"What?" I asked in my mind. What is He referring to? I thought. My mind was fuzzy after such a lack of sleep, having children who never slept without medication, and then still slept only a couple of hours. At one point, my oldest child had gone just shy of four days straight without so much as a nap. My husband and I had been taking shifts watching her, to keep her from hurting herself.

At this point she was six years old and was very limited in her verbal skills. But when I changed her poopy diapers, I would take her hand and try to help her to wipe herself, but she screamed and threw the wipes at me. I would say "This is your job! You need to do this. Big girls go potty on the toilet." All she could say was "No, Mommy's job," over and over again.

As I pondered what God could be referring to, of how to get this break, and how to help my situation, the thought came as a question again from God. "Your degree is in visual communications, is it not? Then why not communicate visually? Use the talents in art and writing that I have blessed you with to bless yourself, your children, and then others."

So—I got up, stopped my crying, and got busy. I stayed up until almost three every night. Some nights I never went to bed. I learned how to use computer programs to scan my art into the computer and how to do layout designs and such, until finally with God's help, I was able to create a step-by-step fully illustrated, 32-page book about how to go potty on the toilet, emphasizing that your parents would still love you and be proud of you, even though you were no longer a baby.

After printing out my book and hand-laminating every page, so that my daughter would not tear it to shreds, I presented it to her. After only one week of using it with her, and this being after years of working with specialists, and everything else I could—she was finally potty-trained. She has never had an accident since. Not too much later my 5-year-old daughter, also with autism and not potty-trained and with her own set of serious problems, picked up the book on her own, looked at it, and copied the steps and toilet-trained herself.

By now, I had mentioned this to a few friends who had children or grandchildren of their own with autism. One of these friends asked to borrow the book and used it with her 9-year-old granddaughter who was autistic and still in diapers. A week later she came to my house crying and thanking me for writing it and telling me that it worked. Her granddaughter was now using the toilet. After sharing this with many people whom it helped, including my younger sister who used it with her nonautistic child, many of them began to encourage me to publish the book.

I said I did not have the time or energy, as I had attempted to publish a different children's book before and knew the time and energy it took and knew the rejection from big companies and such also. Finally, my sister did a search for me and found 10 pages of publishers that she thought might want to publish this book. I looked through the list and felt inspired to give one of the companies a call.

Never realizing that I would be speaking to the owner of the publishing house, assuming I would get a secretary, I called Publication Consultants. I was speaking with Evan Swensen, the owner of the company, but did not know this. I then asked if he could forward the manuscript he had requested to the owner or the person in charge. He just kindly said, "I am the owner and the guy in charge, and I am interested in your book." He was so humble and helpful and friendly that I thought I had been talking to an editor or secretary. I had no idea that he was the owner, editor, secretary, and everything all in one.

Since publishing *No More Diaper for Girls,* I have also published *No More Diaper for Boys* and *The Alaska Sun Turns Silly in the Summertime* through Publication Consultants, and have many other books in the process. My prayers were truly answered. I was not only able to improve my situation, but my children are all toilet-trained, reading above the grade level of their peers, and most people do not even know or recognize that they have autism. They help clean the house and help with our farm and now they are helping clean up chicken poop, instead of wiping their own on the walls of our home. Creating and publishing this book has helped my children, myself, and many others, and I have been very grateful to those who have written to me and told me of their joy and success stories, after using the *No More Diaper* books.

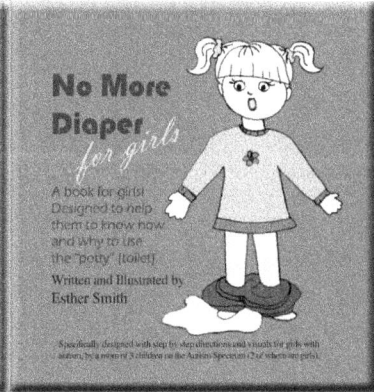

One Last Cast
Evan Swensen

Evan Swensen claims to have the best job in the world—he gets up in the morning, puts on his fishing vest, picks up his fly rod, kisses his wife goodbye, tells her he's going to work—and she believes him.

Bringing One Last Cast to market began when I crossed the border and moved to Alaska in 1957, and since then I've pretty much lived the fantasies of almost all outdoorsmen. I've been the publisher and editor of *Alaska Outdoors* magazine and producer of the *Alaska Outdoors* television show and outdoor videos, and the host of *Alaska Outdoor Radio Magazine*. It was after *Alaska Outdoors Radio Magazine* ran its course and went off the air that the book, *One Last Cast,* was born.

As a private pilot with a float rating, I've logged more than 4,000 hours of flight time in Alaska, in both wheel and float planes. I'm a serious recreation hunter and fisherman, equally comfortable casting a fly rod, and using bait or lures. I live in Alaska and work in the outdoors. I love to fish, hunt, fly, hike, and be in the outdoors.

As publisher of *Alaska Outdoor Magazine*, I had an idea for a book: *The Insiders Guide to Alaska Outdoors*. I wrote inquiry letters to 34 publishers and received 34 rejections. I was disheartened. I thought that I'd have 34 publishers scrambling to be the first to send me a book-publishing contract. I had no idea how tough it was to get a publisher to publish my book.

A few weeks after the last rejection arrived I received a call from a small publisher. They were looking for someone to write *The Hiking Guide to Alaska*. I explained to them that I did a great deal of hiking, but my hiking was to go fishing or hunting. The editor told me that they were considering a *Fishing Guide to Alaska* and ask if I was interested. I was interested and signed a contract for both the fishing and the hiking guide to Alaska.

I signed the contract and proceeded with writing the books. My late wife, Margaret, a great researcher, did the research and I did the writing. We worked on and coauthored the books.

I remember the high we experienced when we received our copies from the publisher. We celebrated our success as writers. The memory lingers today as I remember holding the product of our yearlong labors. It was wonderful.

After the books were published reality set in as we discovered that we were at the bottom of the publishing food chain and our publisher cared little about us. We found that in the contract we had signed away all our rights to the book. We didn't even own the copyright. Our books were not ours—they belonged to the publisher. It was discouraging to know that in our innocence we had relinquished all rights, in all markets—forever.

The small publisher sold to a larger publisher and as bad as the small publisher treated us, the new publisher was so bad they made the first publisher look good. We even had to get a lawyer and threaten the new publisher with legal action to get them to honor the terms of their contract. Dealing with publishers took away a great deal of the thrill of being published authors.

At the conclusion of *Alaska Radio Magazine* I'd end the show each day with these words, "There's just time for one last cast." I then proceeded with a 90-second vignette about one of my Alaska outdoor adventures—mostly adventures with one of my nine children. A few years later we put 120 of those *last cast* stories together and published our book—and we own the copyright.

One Last Cast contains uplifting stories of friends, family, and fun; preserved for posterity.

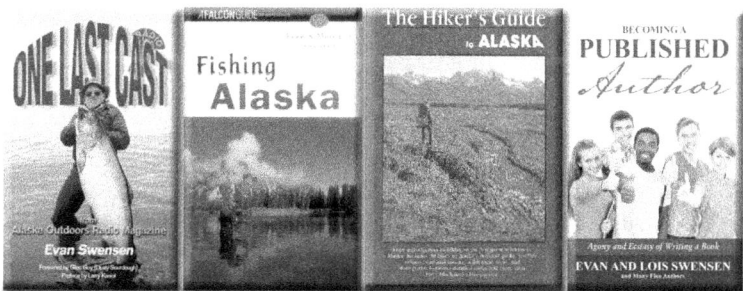

Hearts of Courage
John Tippets

A few years ago I began to realize that my children and grandchildren knew very little about my parents, Joseph and Alta Tippets. They were wonderful people, strong in their faith, but sadly, passed away before their grandchildren were old enough to remember them.

A verse in the Scriptures caught my eye. "Hath this been in your days, or even in the days of your fathers? Tell your children of it, and let your children tell their children of it, and their children another generation" (Joel 1:2–3). And so a project was started—writing about the lives of my parents, searching out information from extended family and personal memories.

The stories gradually became a history of two young people born in the years before World War I and growing up in small Utah towns during the Great Depression. They were married in 1936 while Dad was in the navy, then moved to the western desert for his first job with the Bureau of Air Commerce. By the spring of 1940, Joe and Alta were in Alaska. It was the beginning of an exciting new chapter of their lives, which would bring adventure and great joy, but also incredible challenges.

I gradually became convinced that the events of these Alaska years, including the story of the 1943 Gillam plane crash and Dad's 29-day survival in the snowy wilderness, could provide enough material for a really interesting book. From family letters, newspaper and magazine articles, old photos and several tape recordings of Dad telling the story of the Gillam crash I began to write down details of their 1942–43 experiences. New information soon came from all sorts of unexpected places. *Hearts of Courage* was beginning to take shape, despite time constraints from my full-time job and other obligations over about a four-year span. The research was sometimes sporadic, but there were numerous wonderful discoveries. Some examples:

In an Anchorage Alaska Museum filing cabinet, in a drawer full of old CAA/FAA pictures, I found one of the Annette Island Rock Quarry (p.42). A blasting sound from that quarry on February 10, 1943 caused Harold Gillam to think that they had crashed on Annette. He headed out to look for rescue for his passengers.

A sister of a daughter-in-law had a summer job one year at the Alaska Aviation Heritage Museum. I was in Alaska on a fishing trip when she reached out to me to suggest I come and go through a box of old CAA "Mukluk Telegraph" newsletters. From those I found some really special references to Dad and the story (see the end of this article).

Reading the *Tucsan* ship log at the National Archives gave another perspective as the skipper described the rescue of Joseph Tippets and Sandy Cutting.

Attending a meeting in Juneau, Alaska we visited with Dee Longenbaugh at "The Observatory Books and Maps." She helped us find two 1940s magazine articles where Robert Gebo and Sandy Cutting had recounted their memories of the crash and survival.

From a notebook Dad carried with him at the time, I found names which I traced with two particular successes: I found and visited in Phoenix with Renee Richardson, and a daughter of S. Omer Smith shared her father's personal journal recollections with me. Renee and Omer had been soldiers at Fort Richardson in Anchorage and they were 1943 members of the Latter-Day Saint (LDS) congregation. They had both interacted with Alta when Dad was lost and they each heard Dad tell of his experience when he returned to Anchorage.

As the research process was pretty much finished, my wife, Bonnie, was concerned that we still did not have enough information about Susan Batzer, the new CAA employee who was on the plane headed to Anchorage to start her job. Susan's injuries from the crash were severe and she had passed away on the second day. Bonnie made a sequence of calls and had a new lead at each step. The town clerk in Morristown, South Dakota explained that there was no library, the high school was closed, and there had never been a high school yearbook, but she did have a 90+-year-old father-in-law still living who might be helpful. I realized he was close in age to Susan and in fact, when Bonnie talked to him the next day, he described having been in her class and remembering Susan well. Then from his lead we ultimately found the good picture of Susan (p.35) and the March 1, 1943 letter Joseph wrote to Susan's parents. That letter became Appendix A. Ultimately too, we met Susan's surviving sister in San Diego and the family shared with us a box of special materials, pictures, and articles about her.

There were many more such finds and as a result increasing numbers of details of this event surfaced.

Thinking about putting Dad's story in book form, I had made the decision quite early that this project was going to include a great many pictures and illustrations, perhaps one on almost every page. My model was a sort of *National Geographic* look. *Pictures are worth a thousand words,* and I felt they would be essential to capturing the extreme elements and circumstances of a January Alaska wilderness plane crash. And, because this is almost a Ketchikan legend I was able to enlist local artists, photographers, forest service and museum staff to help me get the pictures and illustrations I felt I needed.

After early efforts to write in the third person a second decision was made; I realized how much of *Hearts of Courage* were really Dad's words. Recognizing that, I decided to do the book, substantially in Dad's first-person voice.

Then there was the process of writing early drafts, having different individuals read those and provide edits and input. Two of those who helped were a retired BYU English professor and Marthy Johnson in Alaska. Trudy Johnson, a church friend in Texas acted as secretary/typist and editor over the years. Even in the last months, each paragraph and each sentence was written and rewritten many, many times. The final and best editor was my wife, Bonnie. It was painful at some points as she wanted to change something I felt strongly about, but in the end we made a product of which we were both proud.

As the form of the book became clearer in my mind, I shared my concepts and drafts with four publishers, two in Alaska and two Utah LDS book publishers. There was interest from three of those, the dropout was Deseret Book. Publication Consultants was introduced to me by J. L. McCarrey III, whose parents, Judge "Mac" McCarrey and his wife, Cora had been close Alaska friends of my parents from the 1940s.

Evan Swensen (Publication Consultants) was an exceptionally good fit both with his understanding of Alaska and of the publishing industry, and also because he saw the labor of love of creating a legacy of my parents that this was for me. Evan was a straight shooter and gave sound suggestions. He told me the standard industry formats, cover designs, content layouts, and so forth. He was clear about the fact that I was less likely to ever have a profitable product with the pictures on every page, and I could get a better cost and perhaps some other benefits if we printed in China. Much of his advice I chose not to follow, but we made a good team as I sat beside him for many hours at his computer as each page of the book was carefully constructed.

The product that became ready to go to print was one I was very pleased with and I hope he was as well. The cover by Terry Pyles is impressive and well captures the moments before the crash; the wonderful Chip Porter photographs, and other pictures and illustrations blend with the narrative and readers get a sense beyond what text can offer.

I'm a bit biased but *Hearts of Courage* was everything I had hoped for. I had decided it was important for me to have all of the ownership and control rights. Evan willingly provided his skills in design and layout and bringing the book into reality while allowing me to technically self-publish. We then did a first printing, which sold out pretty quickly.

At some point early after the book was released I read an article in the *Wall Street Journal* that described three book genres or themes which have special appeal to American readers. Those were "man against nature", "polar survival" and "maritime." I surmised that "aviation" was likely equivalent to maritime and I realized how *Hearts of Courage* really had all three of those elements. Plus, for good measure, it included a love story and the role of a strong faith in God. It was clear that almost all who might learn of *Hearts of Courage* and read it, were going to enjoy it.

Many of the stories in this book for Evan and Lois will largely end at the point of the author's getting the book published, but for *Hearts of Courage* I do want to describe several wonderful experiences that have occurred as a consequence of the book's being on the market.

In early 2008, I was preparing to retire after a 42+-year association with American Airlines, the last 17+ of that tenure as the president and CEO of the American Airlines Credit Union. As one form of a retirement gift, the curator of American's C.R. Smith Museum arranged an extremely professional *Hearts of Courage* exhibit funded by Credit Union friends and vendors. The exhibit was on display at that museum for a year and then went to an Idaho history museum in Boise (home of the Morrison-Knudsen Company, owners of the airplane in the story).

Next year, 2013, 70 years after the events of the story and 100 years after my Dad's birth, that impressive exhibit will be on display at the Museum of Idaho in Idaho Falls; just a few miles from Arimo, where Joseph Tippets was born.

In a sequence of people learning about *Hearts of Courage* I was introduced to the dean of fine arts at Brigham Young University who in turn arranged for me to meet with a BYU TV producer. Bonnie had always felt there should be a BYU connection, in part because in 1967, the year before he died, Dad was recognized with a BYU honorary doctorate degree for his years of public service. And Bonnie was right: the producer with student actors and staff did a *Hearts of Courage: The Story of Joseph and Alta Tippets* documentary as part of their *Inspiring Lives* series. The program has aired many times on BYU TV over the past couple of years, and I hear regularly from someone who has been thrilled in watching it.

And there have been a number of special people with connections to those times that I have met or had contact with: Leonard Olsen, living on Wrangell Island in Alaska, was one of the U.S. Coast Guard reservists who was on the *Tucsan* and rescued Dad and Sandy Cutting. "We took them on board, gave them clean and dry clothes, warmed and fed them pork chops," he described. From Leonard's wife, Josie, I have received copies of pictures taken on board the *Tucsan* of Leonard and Carl Dudler, the two who were in the rowboat on February 3, 1943.

Bill Lofholm, nearing 100 years old in Boise, Idaho, had worked in the 1940s as a Morrison-Knudsen employee alongside Joseph Tippets on many airport projects in Alaska. He was scheduled to be on that plane January 5, 1943, but he had problems getting to Seattle and arrived too late. He went by the hangar and saw that the plane had left.

Fred Hill was responsible for organizing the shore party of the U.S. Coast Guard to go back into the wilderness to search for Dewey Metzdorf and

Robert Gebo after Dad and Cutting had been found. In 2009 at his home on Whidby Island in Washington State he described his unhappiness when he learned that Joe Tippets and Sandy Cutting would be going with them. "We were just going to find two dead men," he said, "and these two going with me might die as well ..."

Two girls, Beverly and Donna Sainsbury, were 8 and 10 years old in the LDS Anchorage Branch during the time when Dad was lost. They remember it well today. *"... As everyone was fasting and praying and your mother kept saying 'He is alright and will come home.' Her faith probably carried the whole branch. But it did happen and of course everyone was overjoyed."* — Beverly

And, sharing the *Hearts of Courage* story in a Sunday School class, a son of my cousin Linda learned of Ben Lofgrens personal journal account where he described being present at the house in Anchorage when Alta learned the plane was missing. *" ... My task in Joe's absence was to see that Alta and her small son were safe and comforted ... On that day I left work and walked about a mile to the Tippets home and found the family excited that Joe would soon be there ... the phone rang. Joe's boss wanted to talk to me ... told me to break the news that the plane was lost somewhere ... We all knelt in the bedroom to pray, I left about 11 p.m. with the storm still raging outside.*

"The process went on for a week, then two ... and still no trace or whereabouts of the pilot and passengers. But the newspapers were full of the story— all very frank and brutal in stating the slight chance of there being any survivors. Finally I had to agree; there was little possibility that any could yet be alive. Much as we hope and pray, there are the cruel realities of life. But Alta could not be consoled ... Joe was out there alive, and someone had to find him ... On the 29th day word was received Joe had been found."

I do presentations of *Hearts of Courage* for different audiences about once a month. At those occasions and in phone calls and emails, I constantly get feedback about the story and how its message of courage, faith, and prayer, of perseverance in the face of adversity is even today continuing to impact hearts and minds of those who hear and read it.

Dad once described how reluctant he was to consider that God had intervened to preserve his life. He just felt that there were far too many good, decent, and innocent people losing their lives in those times; their families had prayed for them, they had hopes and dreams and would have been productive members of society. But, he said, God might have done so "if it might be for no other reason that my life has been preserved, except that I should tell my story so that others might be inspired to persevere in the face of adversity." That is why I will share it today.

And now, 70 years since those times and that experience, we are continuing to tell Dad's story in a book, in a TV documentary, in a museum exhibit, and in luncheon and dinner presentations to interested groups, hopefully inspiring and encouraging readers and listeners as Joseph Tippets wished and because he felt it could have been the reason his life was spared.

> "We all remember the almost incredulous joy and amazement we experienced on February 3 upon hearing that two survivors had been found, including our good friend and coworker, Joseph H. Tippets. After a month of privation and suffering, the fact that even four of the six on board the ill-fated plane survived the long, miserable month almost taxes our imagination, and proves indeed that faith and hope and courage and endurance have tangible rewards.
>
> "The age of miracles is not past!"
>
> Marshall C. Hoping, Alaska Regional Manager
> Civil Aeronautics Administration
> Muluk Telegraph, March 1943

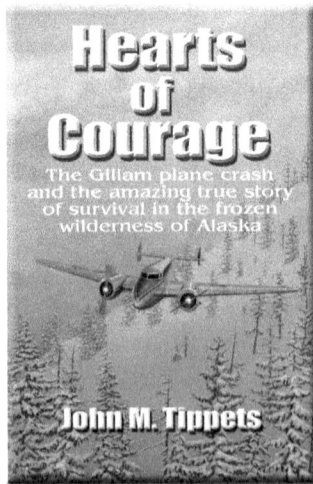

One Author's Trip to Publication
Carol V. Weishampel, Ed.D.

Writing is a passion, like an itch, that can't be ignored. My early writing attempts were personal and secretive. I hid notes and short passages scribbled on yellow legal pads in file drawers, and lost incentive. Publication was foreign, scary, and impossibly out of reach. While teaching art, I became involved with a school writing project that encouraged me to write and illustrate a children's book. The school district printed my little book in paperback. With a "real" book in hand, I was hooked.

No writer's groups or conferences were available to me, but that itch to write had to be scratched, so in secret I began to write what I knew; my family of 12 kids. I had adopted ten of the children as a single parent. Oh, I had stories to tell. Today, that genre is known as a memoir. I thought I was writing excerpts from journals. With much misgiving I contacted a publisher who, for a fee, edited and published my book, *Grandma's on the Go.* Encouraged by seeing a book with my name on the cover, I pulled out old notes for two other nonfiction books, which were published by the same publisher. None of the books sold well, although I spoke when I could and held signings.

I was nervous about speaking, but enjoyed the challenge. Book signings were fun, too, but I soon learned that I am not a good sales person. I developed an elevator pitch for each book, and although I could engage a potential buyer in conversation, I could not get most to buy. Low sales didn't stop me from writing.

Kids grown, retired, rejuvenated and raring to go, I planned my first

RV trip from Texas to Alaska in 2002. Alaska had tugged at my heart from the time I learned that the Alaska Highway had been built in the year of my birth. I would celebrate my 60th birthday by driving the Alcan. This would be a trip of a lifetime. I was denying growing older and gray, but I could not write with my hands on the wheel. I could not jot down ideas that flashed through my head so I carried a small tape recorder that could be activated while I drove. A camera and computer accompanied me. The recorder and photographs, and a collection of picture postcards and brochures enhanced my daily journal. That summer and the following summer I volunteered at a Christian youth camp in Wasilla and a church in Fairbanks.

The journals from these two trips resulted in *Grandma's Ultimate Road Trip, Texas to Alaska* which was published in Texas. By 2006, I couldn't stay away from Alaska any longer and returned to volunteer. This time I carried a digital recorder. As the miles and majestic scenery slipped by, a fiction story began to slip into my consciousness. A road trip to Alaska would be the vehicle. My wonderful memories of Alaskan people and places would enhance the plot. Although recorded in no sequence, my thoughts assembled into scene and sequel, conflict and resolution, romance and mystery. By the return trip I had a rough outline of *Venture in Faith, Texas to Alaska*. Through my travels I had met another author who had published with Publication Consultants. She, too, was from the Lower 48 and explained that Evan would consider manuscripts with an Alaska theme, even though the author was not an Alaska resident.

I submitted the manuscript and was pleased with the reception I received. Evan asked for my input for the cover design. I sent him my ideas and liked his cover; however, he had a motor home in the design that was different from the one I described in the story, and I mentioned that a bear was prominent in the plot. Evan quickly tweaked the cover to an RV that matched the story and added a bear that "came out from the bushes." I was most pleased.

A year later Publication Consultants published my children's book, *Loon's Necklace*, which I had illustrated. This little book has even sold well in Texas although we do not have loons.

I've had book signings in Anchorage and surrounding areas that were set up by Publication Consultants, shared a booth at the Palmer Fair, the Delta Fair and at the farmers' market. Promotion time has been limited due to volunteer obligations.

I had one disastrous publishing experience which I'll share to warn writers about "editors and predators." I contracted with a local Texas publisher to edit and publish a novel set in Texas, thinking that his hype about local promotion would be an advantage. I paid a fee for editing, printing, and promotion, but the first proof, which took several months, had excessive errors that were not my errors. I was shocked that my name had been misspelled. The cover did not match the plot. I marked pages of errors and returned the proof. Promises of a cleaned-up proof dragged into two years of excuses. I took him to small claims court, but settled in mediation. He would provide a new cover and make all necessary corrections. Many months later the "new" proof was no improvement over the old. After three years of irritation, I took his company to mediation again, and demanded my money back and all rights to my manuscript. I received the rights to the book, but no monetary award. Satisfied, knowing this was the best I could do, I had the book published online. I had learned a very costly lesson: make sure the publisher and/or editor I chose was reputable.

Six summer trips by RV to volunteer in the majestic state of Alaska has qualified me as a "six-six." Six months in Texas. Six months in Alaska. I dream of experiencing a winter holed up in a cozy cabin with a computer and notes for another tale.

Alaska Wolff Pack
Margaret Wolff

Writing the story of my life was not a decision I made, it was something that I had to do. I was blessed with such a remarkable family and friends that it was imperative to get their lives down on paper. At first I didn't plan to get my book published; I just expected to print several copies for family and friends. In order to get started I retired early—I was only 70—from a job I really enjoyed. Then I waited several months before beginning; I was afraid I would discover that I couldn't remember everything or that the right words wouldn't come. Once I was brave enough to begin, there was no stopping.

I thought I could write only on paper, so with pen in hand, I began. You should have seen my writing! There were more words crossed out than there were left on the paper and there were arrows pointing everywhere. One quickly needed a road map to read it, as there were dozens of notes and symbols everywhere.

My daughter Shianne—who can spell—replied, "I can't correct this! I can't even read it!" She suggested that I at least try to write on the computer. What a difference! I want to use a different word—backspace and write the new word. I want to put something in a different place—delete and rewrite it where I want it. I want to add or subtract something—easy. When I'm done, I'm done; I don't have to type what I've written. It's even readable!

My brother Jim placed all the pictures and captions at the beginning of each chapter. He suggested it would be easier for readers if I had a list of characters so that they could look back to see just who Snuffy or somebody else is. I followed his suggestion but I called it a list of heroes and heroines. With the exception of myself that's what they all are, every one of them. My husband lost his life saving mine; later my son risked his life saving mine; my other son was murdered while coming to the aid of others, and it goes on and on. I could tell you heroic and wonderful things about all of them, but that would be another book. I regret that I couldn't put all the heroes and heroines that are in my life in the book. All the wonderful absent people and the terrific people I've gotten to know since are always in my memory and in my heart.

My fears about not being able to remember were unfounded. When I began each new chapter, I had a very sketchy idea of only a few of the things I wanted to write. Once I was at the computer and began, I was flooded with memories, thoughts, and feelings that I hadn't remembered in years. I became so immersed in the time and place I was writing about, that if asked the date I might have answered something like June 1969. Usually I know the present date and the day of the week that all birthdays and holidays will fall on; but then it was hard for me to come back to the present place and time. Writing my story was like reliving my life! I paused to bolster my defense before writing about the loss of my loved ones, but the continuing gratitude for the years that I'd had with them overshadowed my loss. I encourage everyone to write their autobiographies, then all the adventures, the fun and hilarity, the sad times, the relationships, the excitement and challenges are always there for you and your readers. It's one of life's greatest treasures!

Another reward people may receive while writing their autobiography is some sort of a strange connection to the people they're writing about. Several times in the midst of writing I paused to answer the telephone and when I returned to the computer I discovered that the caller was who I had been writing about when the telephone rang. One of the times I was called to be informed that a dear friend (one of my heroines) was critically ill and in the hospital. When I returned her name was the last word that I had written. Another time I was writing about an unexpectedly eventful party my husband and I were giving for friends and the construction guys he was working with, just before we planned to leave so that we could live in the Alaska bush. One of the attending construction workers, who

I hadn't talked to in more than 40 years, happened to see my name in the telephone book and he gave me a call. This happened often enough to make me hopeful that I would hear from others who I had lost contact with, but unfortunately I had no control over the connection. It would be even stranger to be contacted by fictitious story characters. That could be or may not be a good thing.

When my manuscript was complete I printed a few copies. Since by now my daughter had a published book, I decided that I'd give it a try to get mine published too. The first two places I sent the manuscript to replied, "No, thank you." The third place said that they publish only Alaska fiction, but she very kindly suggested that I try Publication Consultants. I can't tell you how glad I am that I followed her suggestion! What an exciting adventure, and how awesome was the help I received! Publication Consultants not only got my manuscript ready, printed, and published at full speed, but they have directed and assisted me in every step of the marketing. From the delightful book-signing party in my home, to all the book signings, webinars, advice, and so much more they have been wonderful! I receive an accounting (and often a check) every month. My daughter's experience with her publisher is totally the opposite and now that she knows what a difference one's publisher makes she would never consider going with them again. I give Publication Consultants' business card to every aspiring author I meet, and there have been many!

Since mine is a true story, there were no decisions about how the plot would proceed. My daughter writes fiction but she does not have that much to say about her plots either. Once she gets started in the general direction, her stories take on a life of their own and take unexpected turns. She wasn't given a choice about how her first novel would end and she didn't know what the ending would be until it ended. She was afraid that she might have to quit in the middle of her second novel if it had taken a direction that she couldn't accept. I know how she feels—in my earlier writings that were fiction, I was carried along for the ride and was unsure of where we were going until we got there. I don't think that there is any writing that is totally fiction anyway. The story may never have happened, but I believe that the experiences, personality, beliefs, and feelings of the author are naturally incorporated. It's like one's child, they are always a part of their parents and their parents are a part of them.

A reward that is greater than all monetary rewards is the way a published book can reach out to people. Being an avid reader, I find that many characters from my favorite books have taken a place in my thoughts and life. It gives me great pleasure to know that the people I love will take a part in the lives of others. The people in my book are too unique to be forgotten! I like to put the business card (which Evan so generously had printed for me) inside the books I sell. It has my telephone number and email address and I welcome every call and message I receive. I want to meet and get to know as many people as I can. I'm pleased that I have received calls and messages from so many places and have had the opportunity to talk to so many people. I told one lady from Vermont that I was going to visit my son in Ohio and she replied. "Oh you mean Timber!" My daughter said that once someone she didn't know told her, "You must be Shianne." To receive a hug from someone you've just met because he or she has read your book is delightful!

In short, if you take the time to write your story you won't regret it. Every minute you spend in doing so pays in a magnitude of joy! If you're fortunate enough to have Publication Consultants as your publisher, congratulations!

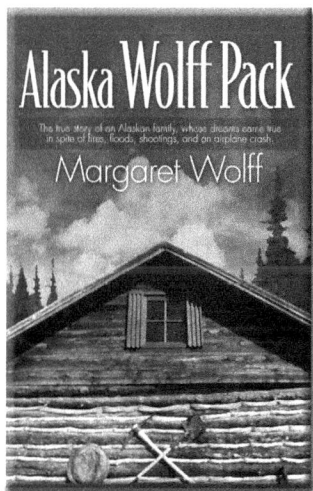

Bringing Your Book To Market

Publication Consultants specializes in publishing the works of authors worldwide. We've been in the publishing business since 1978. We're not only publishers, we're writers, and know many problems confronting writers. How to solve those problems and bring your work to market is our business. Most questions about publishing your book will be answered as you read Bringing Your Book to Market. Although the book describes how we bring your book to market, we also work with writers who do not intend to sell their books, but are publishing for self, family, friends, or business purposes. We can publish your book if you don't intend to sell your book, or if you only want a few copies printed--even only one copy. Publication Consultants produces books and publications of any size, number of pages, and variety of binding and covers. We think there is more to book publishing than just putting ink on paper. Our services include design, typesetting, printing, binding, eBook conversion, and all necessary steps to publish your book, both as a printed book and as an eBook. We take your book from conception to completion and bring your work to market with one of five different programs.

www.ingramcontent.com/pod-product-compliance
Lightning Source LLC
Chambersburg PA
CBHW060832050426
42453CB00008B/664